OLMSTED IN SEATTLE

CREATING A PARK SYSTEM FOR A MODERN CITY

By *JENNIFER OTT*

HistoryLink / Documentary Media

Seattle

OLMSTED IN SEATTLE: CREATING A PARK SYSTEM FOR A MODERN CITY

©2019 by HistoryLink.org. All rights reserved. No part of this book may be reproduced or utilized in any form without the prior written consent of HistoryLink.

HistoryLink
admin@historylink.org
www.historylink.org
(206) 447-8140

Produced by Documentary Media LLC
books@docbooks.com
www.documentarymedia.com
(206) 935-9292

First Edition
Printed in USA

Written by: Jennifer Ott
Editor: Judy Gouldthorpe
Book Design: Jon Cannell Design
Salal and sword fern illustrations: Solvej Cannell
Cover photograph: Dean Forbes
Production Assistants: Edward Daschle, Tori Smith
Editorial Director: Petyr Beck, Documentary Media LLC

ISBN: 978-1-933245-56-0

Distributed by the University of Washington Press
uwapress@uw.edu
(206) 543-4050

Library of Congress Cataloging-in-Publication Data

Names: Ott, Jennifer, 1971- author.
Title: Olmsted in Seattle : creating a park system for a modern city / by Jennifer Ott.
Description: First edition. | Seattle : HistoryLink and Documentary Media, [2019] | Includes bibliographical references and index.
Identifiers: LCCN 2019015483 | ISBN 9781933245560 (alk. paper)
Subjects: LCSH: Olmsted, John Charles, 1852-1920. | Urban landscape architecture—Design and plans—Seattle—History. | Urban parks—Design and plans—Seattle—History. | Landscape architects—United States—Biography. | City planning—Seattle—History. | Olmsted Brothers.
Classification: LCC SB472.7 .O88 2019 | DDC 712/.509797772—dc23
LC record available at https://lccn.loc.gov/2019015483

Page 1: Wading pool at Hiawatha Playfield, 1912.

Page 2: Rustic furnishings along a path in Schmitz Preserve Park, 1910.

CONTENTS

Seattle, view eastward from Elliott Bay, 1896.

PARKS AND THE MODERN AMERICAN CITY

When John Charles Olmsted came to Seattle in April 1903, he found a city materializing before his eyes as if someone had pressed a "fast-forward" button. The Klondike Gold Rush of 1897 opened the floodgates and the population soared from less than 43,000 in 1890 to more than 80,000 in 1900, and was on its way to 237,000 in 1910. The impact of such a rapid increase was felt throughout the city: Housing developments and commercial buildings sprang up on formerly vacant lots and the Elliott Bay shoreline bristled with new piers.

Residents welcomed the development—it was the realization of 50 years of aspirations and hard work—but they also knew a modern American city should be more than just a center of commerce. Civic leaders embraced the public park movement, which had redefined the modern city as a place where architectural and landscape beauty were as essential as railroads and factories. They recognized that to make Seattle a significant city, worthy of acclaim and investment, they needed to develop a park system and "make the city beautiful." To that end, they sought out a notable outside authority with ties to the major cities of the East Coast, which would give the system legitimacy and attract public support.

Hiring the Olmsted Brothers, the nationally acclaimed landscape architects from Brookline,

Massachusetts, was a keen investment in the city's future. The Olmsted name was synonymous with the public park movement. They had played key roles in defining the importance of parks, introducing the idea of urban planning through the development of park systems, and establishing the field of landscape architecture. Bringing John Olmsted to Seattle provided a direct link to the Olmsted projects that had shaped public spaces in Boston, New York, and Washington, D.C.

American cities had negligible differentiation between land uses in the early 19th century. Homes, factories, stores, and transportation facilities intermingled. As the cities grew noisier, more chaotic and crowded, and pollution overwhelmed residents, the need for open space became more apparent. The public squares that often served as the only designated open spaces provided a visual break from surrounding buildings and a place for people to gather or pause away from the bustling marketplaces, but very little attention was paid to any sort of planning or design for them.

Seattle's first plats followed this pattern, but then diverged from the progression seen in eastern cities, where cemeteries were the first formally designed areas that offered city dwellers access to open space. Mount Auburn Cemetery in Cambridge,

Plat of the
Town of Seattle
King County, Washington Territory.

Henry Yesler's Plat of the Town of Seattle, filed in 1853, with part of a
block at 6th and Washington reserved for a public square.

REPLATTED AS
YESLER TERRACE
VOL. 37 PGS 21 - 22 - 22 A

Blocks 45-46-57-58

(≈ 200' 1 inch)

PUBLIC SQUARE

Washington   Street.

Main   Street.

Jackson   Street.

King   Street.

Weller   Street.

Lane   Street.

Seattle   Commercial Street   Second Street   Third Street   Fourth Street   Fifth Street   Sixth   Seventh   Eighth   Ninth   Tenth Street

Tide Lands Vol. 2. P. 28 - 29 & 30

East end of Plat.

Replatted Vol. 1 Pg. 93

Replatted Vol. 1 P. 169

INSTRUMENT AFFECTI
RECORDED "73012202

N
S

Explanation.
Blocks 240 by 256 feet including an alley running North & South of 16 feet wide. Lots 60 ft. by 120
varying according to Plat. Streets running due East and West & North & South 66 ft. wide.

This day personally appeared D. S. Maynard. and acknowledged the within to be a true Copy
of the Plat of the Town of Seatle, in King County, Washington Territory and that the same is
in accordance with hiss free will, wishes and desire of which he is proprietor.
                                        Seattle May 23ᵈ 1853.
                                                H. L. Yesler.

Recorded in the Records of King County
Washington Territory in Vol. "A" Page 6.
Transcribed Vol. 1. of Deeds, Page 86.
Re-recorded (per order County Com's at the
Feby Term of Court 1875) in this plat Book
Mch 18th, 1875.
        S. C. Harris
                Draughtsman.

Massachusetts, Laurel Hill Cemetery in Philadelphia, and Green-Wood Cemetery in Brooklyn opened in the 1830s. As they became popular with city dwellers, they increased support for public park development. At about the same time, Boston converted the Common from a shared livestock grazing area into a public park.

Seattle's smaller population in the 1850s to 1880s, ample open space, and easy access to waterways diminished the need to make its cemetery or other spaces into formal parks, so city leaders focused on economic development as they built the fledgling settlement into a bustling market town. At the same time, the desire to "keep up" with other American cities and the steady stream of newcomers from Eastern and Midwestern cities ensured that Seattleites were aware of the evolution of thinking about city parks. Newspapers across Washington Territory regularly mentioned parks being developed in larger cities and noted the reservation of lands for public parks in plats being filed for new Washington towns.

The public discourse was shaped by park advocates who wrote about the beneficial influence parks had on public health and moral character. In the highly polluted cities of the 19th century, where skies were clogged with smoke and other pollutants, the trees, shrubs, and lawns in parks served as "the lungs of the city," creating refuges of fresh air. The advocates also argued that parks provided refined imitations of nature, claiming that exposure to them would improve people's character, regardless of their socioeconomic

status. Early landscape architect Andrew Jackson Downing wrote in 1848, "[Parks] will be better preachers of temperance than temperance societies, better refiners of national manners than dancing schools, and better promoters of general good-feeling than any lectures on the philosophy of happiness.' "

Sentiments like this reflect the influence of the Romantics on American attitudes toward nature. What had once been seen as something separate from humans, to be conquered or feared, became something humans were part of and that they could turn to for restoration. Early landscape designers, such as Downing and Frederick Law Olmsted Sr., also brought their experiences touring European estates and public gardens, particularly in England, to the United States, further emphasizing the beneficial relationship between humans and nature rather than their separation. Even on the West Coast, where the human imprint on the landscape was much less visible and where what they perceived as "untamed wilderness" was much closer at hand, the influence of the Romantics was felt and attitudes toward the natural world evolved.

Few exemplified these ideas better than Olmsted and Calvert Vaux in their designs for Central Park in Manhattan and Prospect Park in Brooklyn and in their writings. In their 1868 report to Brooklyn's park board they discussed how parks could counteract the negative effects of working conditions:

There is no doubt that the more intense intellectual activity, which prevails equally in the library, the work shop and the counting room, makes tranquilizing recreation more essential to continued health and

Lithograph of Philadelphia's Laurel Hill Cemetery, ca. 1848.

Mount Auburn Cemetery, Cambridge, Massachusetts.

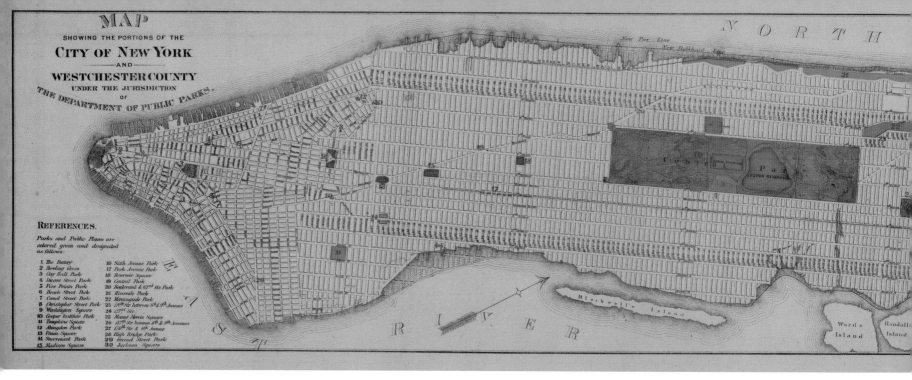

Map of Manhattan, showing Central Park in relation to the crowded downtown district at the tip of the island.

strength than until lately it generally has been. *Civilized men . . . are growing more and more subject to other and more insidious enemies to their health and happiness, and against these the remedy and preventive can not be found in medicine or in athletic recreations, but only in sunlight and such forms of gentle exercise as are calculated to equalize the circulation and relieve the brain.*

Olmsted also believed that public parks provided more than just moral and health benefits. He thought a well-designed public space could bring people together who would not normally interact, thereby strengthening the community and American democracy. In 1870, he claimed to have seen this himself:

> *Consider that the New York Park and the Brooklyn Park are the only places in those associated cities where . . . you will find a body of Christians coming together, and with an evident glee in the prospect of coming together, all classes largely represented, with a common*

purpose, not at all intellectual, competitive with none, disposing to jealousy and spiritual or intellectual pride toward none, each individual adding by his mere presence to the pleasure of all others, all helping to the greater happiness of each. You may thus often see vast numbers of persons brought closely together, poor and rich, young and old, Jew and Gentile. I have seen a hundred thousand thus congregated, and I assure you that though there have been not a few that seemed a little dazed, as if they did not quite understand it, and were, perhaps, a little ashamed of it, I have looked studiously but vainly among them for a single face completely unsympathetic with the prevailing expression of good nature and lightheartedness.

The largest and most influential of the early city parks was Central Park in New York City. Designed by Olmsted & Vaux in 1858, it encompassed an enormous tract of land located just to the north of the urban core of the city. It provided open space on a scale to match the city that was growing toward it

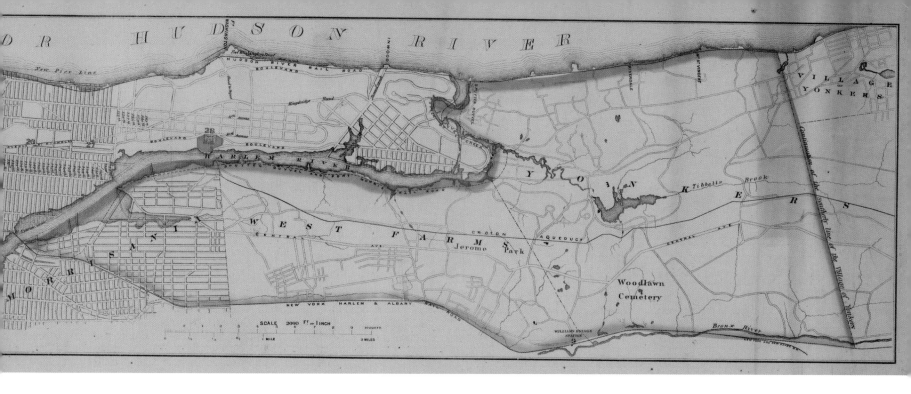

from the south end of Manhattan. It offered an oasis of green and provided space for a variety of uses, from organized games to quiet contemplation. The park soon attracted crowds of people to picnic on "The Green," wander the paths of "The Ramble," or ice skate on the lake. Large parks began to proliferate in urban areas across the country. An article in Olympia's *Washington Standard* newspaper in 1860 noted that "Boston has caught the Central Park fever, and is engaged in preparing a Public Garden at the expense of $190,000." After the Civil War, a number of new large city parks were developed, including Prospect Park in Brooklyn (1866), Golden Gate Park in San Francisco (1870), and Forest Park in St. Louis (1876).

It was not long, however, before park planning grew to include city planning through the development of park systems. Olmsted was at the forefront of this shift and helped establish standards

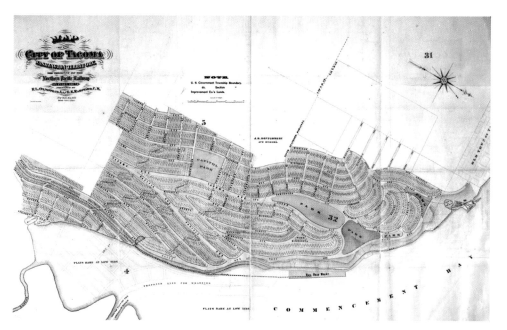

Although he didn't visit Tacoma, Frederick Law Olmsted Sr. was hired to design a city plan for the newly designated terminus of the Northern Pacific Railway, in 1873. His (unused) plan featured curvilinear streets across the hillside above the bay and several parks.

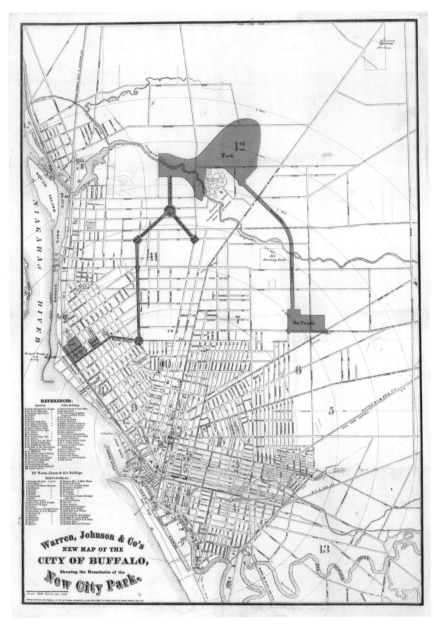

Map of the Buffalo, New York, park system designed by Olmsted & Vaux. It was the first plan for a public park system in the United States.

for park systems through a number of influential projects in cities across the United States. In their early work on Central Park and Prospect Park, Olmsted & Vaux had realized that a single enormous site was not adequate to meet the needs of the whole city. In the case of Central Park, the park was out of reach for some, especially tenement dwellers living in the densely populated districts of lower Manhattan, who could not afford the time or carfare needed to visit it. By 1868, Olmsted & Vaux had developed the idea of parkways. They envisioned these drives extending out from parks into the surrounding neighborhoods, providing

> *a series of ways designed with express reference to the pleasure with which they may be used for walking, riding, and the driving of carriages; for rest, recreation, refreshment, and social intercourse; and . . . so arranged that they will be conveniently accessible from every dwelling house and allow its occupants to pass from it to distant parts of the town.*

The culmination of this concept was the park and boulevard system, introduced by Olmsted & Vaux in Buffalo, New York, in 1870. Parks connected to each other via parkways could provide easy access to nature, opportunities for recreation, and places to promenade and gather and could help provide an overarching vision for the organization of a city's business and residential districts. The Olmsted firms' work on park systems over the next several decades changed how cities thought about parks and how they could be used to shape city development.

By the end of the 19th century, as Seattle began to look in earnest for ways to develop its parks, it was well established that cities needed parks and that parkways played an important role in providing access for all of a city's residents to open space and natural beauty. In 1900, Superintendent Frank Little, City Engineer R. H. Thomson, and city council member James A. James went to Chicago to attend the Good Road Convention and the Irrigation Congress. They toured several cities while in the East and urged the city council upon their return to make

> intelligent use of every opportunity to acquire proper and suitable parks and park driveways or park boulevards. We are convinced that the growth of the city is being materially retarded by the lack of such driveways as are common through many, if not all, of our Eastern cities. This is a matter of more than ordinary importance. A great increase in mileage of good healthful driveways around our lakeshores, we believe to be one of the imperative demands of the day.

If Seattle wanted to become the city of its leaders' dreams, it would be essential that they develop a park system to serve the recreational and social needs of the community and provide a framework for the city's future growth.

When Seattle's park board succeeded in hiring the Olmsted Brothers to design a city park system in 1903, they not only ensured that they would achieve their immediate goal of making Seattle a modern city with parks on a par with those of Chicago, Atlanta, and Louisville, but they also laid the foundation for a park system that would serve the city into the next century, shaping its development and establishing a common understanding among residents that continues today: a livable city must provide access for all to beautiful, restorative places.

View across Hoyt Lake, Delaware Park in Buffalo, New York.

Delaware Avenue in Buffalo, view to the north from North Street.

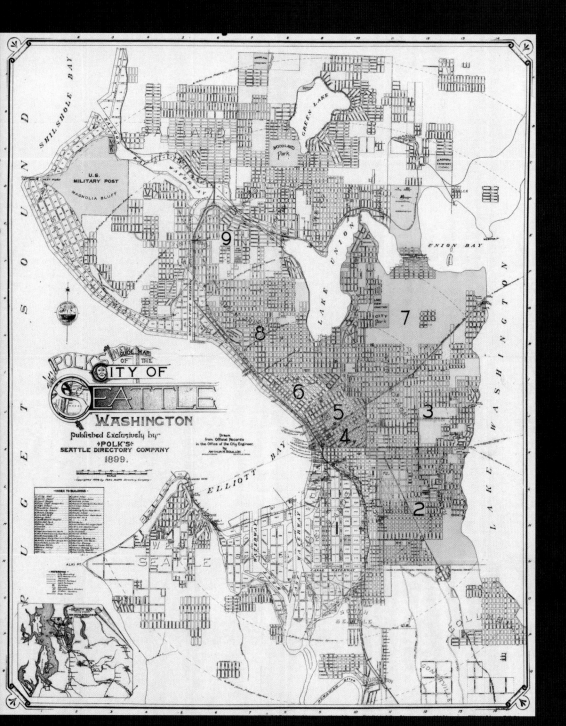

Map of Seattle in 1899 showing incorporated area (shaded) and platted streets.

CHAPTER 1

FROM DENNY PARK TO THE SCHWAGERL PLAN

In 1903, Seattle had everything it needed to become the city of its founders' dreams—a hinterland teeming with resources, a deepwater harbor, proximity to Asia and Alaska, rail connections to the Midwest and East Coast, and a spectacular natural setting. But the city was in disorder and disarray. Street regrades in the downtown core made them a muddy mess. Construction sites abounded as numerous new buildings filled the city blocks stretching north from Pioneer Square, the city's oldest neighborhood. Ships crowded the piers jutting out from the central waterfront's shore. Property owners in the outlying neighborhoods sometimes set their lots afire to clear the undergrowth and logging refuse so they could build homes and businesses, often filling the air with smoke. Sanitary fills (a euphemism for garbage dumps) in low or swampy areas, often near waterways, created level land in a city of hills. The business of the

waterfront relied on a makeshift elevated platform of wooden-planked streets and railroad trestles because efforts to finance a seawall had repeatedly failed. In the absence of zoning laws, officials had little control over how the city grew. Outside of downtown, property owners platted subdivisions haphazardly along the lakes and on the hills that surrounded the city center.

There were efforts to catch up with the growth and build essential infrastructure during these boom years. The new municipal Cedar River water system brought clean water and effective fire protection to the city. A rudimentary sewer system shunted filth out of the streets and into pipes. Streetcar lines increased mobility around the city. City Engineer R. H. Thomson brought some order to the waterfront by insisting that piers built after the Great Fire of 1889 conform to a uniform alignment and hammering

View south from Pike Street and 2nd Avenue, Seattle, 1878.

Informal Recreation Spaces

Before public parks were established, people in Seattle found a variety of places to picnic, swim, ramble, or play games. Native people gathered at numerous sites along the sound and lakes to play *slahal* (a gambling game), race canoes, and otherwise enjoy the natural beauty. A number of these places, often also the sites of villages or camping spots, would become city parks, including Leschi, Washington, Ravenna, Seward, and Green Lake Parks. Non-Native settlers were also drawn to the water. Budlong's Boat House on the central waterfront rented small boats for recreational use. J. Willis Sayre recounted in his book *This City of Ours* how kids used the hull of the schooner *Windward*, anchored at the foot of Columbia Street, as a swimming platform. On the forested edges of the city, property owned by timber companies, such as Puget Mill Company, or homesteaders, was also often used for picnicking and excursions.

The Windward *(on left in photo) was a salvaged barque anchored at the foot of Columbia Street and used as a breakwater.*

out an agreement with the Great Northern Railroad to build a tunnel under downtown and shift some of their operations off the central waterfront.

One element of city building remained stymied despite more than a decade of effort: a park system. The city had several parks—Denny and Kinnear Parks north of downtown, City Park (later Volunteer Park) on Capitol Hill, and Woodland Park on the northern outskirts—along with a handful of small squares and triangles at street intersections. The city also owned other tracts that would later be incorporated into the park system. These included the land that would become Cal Anderson, Washington, Jefferson, Dearborn, and Rodgers Parks.

The parks were developed to varying degrees and were popular with residents, but they garnered more than their fair share of criticism. In 1893, park commissioners had passed a resolution that City Park should be sold to provide funds for acquiring "a larger and more suitable tract for park purposes" on Lake Washington because the City Park tract was too dry, too hard to reach from downtown, and too small for a "driving park." In 1903, an editorial in *The Seattle Republican* bemoaned the "keep off the grass" signs in city parks and called for changes so children could romp on the grass and in playgrounds. Neighbors complained about the nuisance of kids playing baseball on the undeveloped city-owned land adjacent to the reservoir near Broadway High School. The open, empty lot was a magnet for misbehavior. An attempt to create a plan for a park system that would serve the city into the future was made in 1892

Scene in Kinnear Park.

Denny Park, 1904.

but stymied by economic depression in the wake of the Panic of 1893 and a host of other factors, including a spectacularly ineffective Board of Park Commissioners.

A decade later, circumstances had changed completely. The economy was booming, exponential growth gave substance to years of predictions of impending cityhood, and the City Beautiful movement was underway. City Beautiful provided a philosophical underpinning and a road map for civic betterment that emphasized the need for city park systems and popularized the idea of bringing in outside experts to consult with municipal officials. With the appointment of a new slate of prominent

and effective park commissioners in 1902, the city was ready when the opportunity arose to bring John Olmsted to Seattle. His 1903 visit to Seattle would be the beginning of a nearly four-decade relationship between the city and his firm, Olmsted Brothers, Landscape Architects. During that time, Olmsted and his firm would guide the planning and design of the foundation of Seattle's phenomenal park system and, in the process, shape the character of the city.

Born in 1852, John Olmsted was the son of John Hull and Mary Perkins Olmsted and the nephew of Frederick Law Olmsted Sr. After the death of John Hull Olmsted in 1857, Frederick married John's

Private Parks

Private parks sprouted up along the shore of Lake Washington in the 1890s as streetcar lines extended out from downtown to ferry docks on the lake. Property owners developed the parks at Madison Park, Madrona, and Leschi to attract potential residents for their newly platted subdivisions, boost streetcar ridership, and provide pleasant surroundings for the ferry landings. Leschi Park was typical of the private parks. It was developed by the Lake Washington Railroad Company in 1889. The dock served passengers for the ferry *Leschi*, which ran between the park and Mercer Island and Medina, and offered launches, rowboats, and canoes for rent. Other amusements included a roller skating rink, a bandstand, and a dance pavilion, along with well-tended gardens. Guy Phinney applied the same model to his estate on the hill above Green Lake, building a streetcar line and developing a bathing beach on the lake and attractions like ballfields and picnic grounds on the uplands.

Leschi Park boat landing and Anderson Steamboat Company's ferry dock, ca. 1910.

17

Frederick Law Olmsted Sr., ca. 1895.

mother, becoming John's stepfather. John traveled the country with his stepfather and showed an early aptitude for observation of the natural world. In 1864, he spent the summer with his family in California, exploring much of Yosemite. While there, he was exposed to the grand scenery that the senior Olmsted would so eloquently describe when justifying the preservation of Yosemite for future generations in his *Yosemite and the Mariposa Grove: A Preliminary Report, 1865.* John Olmsted kept a journal on the trip and sketched the flora and fauna in its pages, developing his knowledge of the natural world and observational skills that would serve him throughout his career.

The younger Olmsted studied at Yale's Sheffield Scientific School, graduating in 1875 with a bachelor of science degree. He joined his stepfather's firm and worked with him on a variety of projects, including the world's fair in Chicago, Biltmore, the Vanderbilts' estate in North Carolina, and a number of public park projects. After Olmsted Sr. retired, John formed a new firm with his half-brother and cousin, Frederick Law Olmsted Jr. (known familiarly as Rick) in 1897.

When Olmsted arrived in Seattle in 1903, the park board took him on a tour of the existing parks that the city had managed to develop. In 1875, the territorial legislature amended Seattle's charter to explicitly allow the city "to purchase or condemn and enter upon, and take any lands within or without its territorial limit for public squares, streets, parks, commons, cemeteries, hospital grounds . . . and to inclose [sic], ornament and improve the same . . . and for these purposes may levy and collect special taxes." By then, the city had grown to around 2,000 people

Giant Sequoia trees in the Mariposa Grove, Yosemite National Park, ca. 1900.

John Olmsted's drawing of a monarch butterfly, made during his childhood stay in California, 1864-1865.

and some industry had developed in the vicinity of today's Pioneer Square. The city purchased some land with its new authority, including a large tract on today's Capitol Hill that would become Volunteer Park, but generally speaking, there was still ample undeveloped space in close proximity and the

John Charles Olmsted, 1907.

city prioritized infrastructure projects that would encourage economic development.

The first city park was donated by David and Louisa Denny in 1884. After originally donating the land in about 1864 for a city cemetery, the Dennys decided to plat the remainder of land they owned surrounding it as a residential neighborhood, and they wanted the cemetery parcel to serve as a park, so they redonated it as such. The bodies were exhumed and reburied on the city's tract on Capitol Hill (then known as Renton Hill), which was named Washelli Cemetery. Denny Park, which a later city official described as "in the woods, surrounded by tall timber and dense undergrowth, and accessible only by ordinary country roads," provided a nucleus of public open space from which the city's park system would grow.

In 1890, the city charter was changed again. A Department of Parks was formed and a park fund established, made up of monies from park bonds, city council allocations, and a property tax, the rate of which would be determined each year, but could not exceed $1 per $1,000 in assessed value. The Board of Park Commissioners could use the money to purchase land (with city council approval) and develop and maintain parks. All park system management fell under their purview. The five park commissioners each received an annual salary of $300 and served five-year terms. At the first meeting of the new board, chairman Daniel Jones, a local land developer, began with a statement on parks and their role in the life of the city, recorded verbatim in the minutes. Jones expounded, "No City is equipped without some grounds for public resort. . . . If we have faith in the future greatness of our City we must use all our efforts to secure while we may, such lands as will be adequate to the wants of a Large City." Jones warned that if they waited until the city grew to a population of 500,000, they would not be able to "buy a lost opportunity."

Edward O. Schwagerl

Edward O. Schwagerl was born in Würzburg, Bavaria, in 1842 and immigrated to the United States in 1854. He worked as a landscape architect and park superintendent in cities across the country, including Cleveland, Omaha, and St. Louis, before coming to the Northwest in 1885. While in St. Louis, he laid out Lindell Boulevard and designed Vandeventer Place. He established a nursery business at Kingston and then became superintendent for Tacoma's park system in 1886. While there, he designed Wright Park and Point Defiance Park. After serving as Seattle's park superintendent from 1892 to 1895, he would work as a landscape architect for private clients until his death in 1910.

Tacoma's Wright Park had a number of rustic features, including this wooden bridge over Bird Lake, shown here in about 1910.

Jones refuted concerns about taxation by referencing the experience of New York, where the development of Central Park increased property values enough that new tax revenue covered park acquisition and development costs, with funds to spare. He called for the hiring of a "thoroughly competent Landscape Gardener to examine the lay of the land in and around our City to designate certain available lands best adapted for park purposes as well as certain streets for Drives and Boulevards connecting these lands to afford opportunity for pleasure driving." By having such a plan, Jones believed, no effort or money would be wasted.

In calling for an expert, Jones acknowledged the complete absence of park management experience among the commissioners. The board represented the business class of the community: wealthy, white, and property-owning. Jones was a real estate agent, and the other board members had similar backgrounds: businessman William E. Burgess, Merchants National Bank vice president and real

Path in Denny Park, 1909.

estate investor Abram Barker, developer and business owner William E. Bailey, and contractor Otto Ranke. The commissioners advised the city on parks matters with the understanding that what was good for the economic development of the city was also good for the community.

The process of developing Seattle's parks during this time was not smooth. The park board first hired landscape gardener James Taylor to be park superintendent and asked him to prepare a plan of action. Compared to the lofty goals of Jones' speech, Taylor's plan was quite mundane. He recommended construction of a greenhouse, getting as much manure (for fertilizing planting beds) as possible, and improving more of the parkland already owned by the city. He briefly looked beyond the nuts-and-bolts issues, however, and opined, "But it is not for such [tax] returns that public parks are established and maintained. Their object is to provide natural scenery, pleasant walks, retired nooks and green lawns. Something to draw the people to the fresh air and to allure them, for the time being, from all business or domestic cares."

Unfortunately, Taylor had difficulty maintaining good relations with the park employees and left in a huff in April 1892. The park board turned to a more established park superintendent, Edward O. Schwagerl. He was hired explicitly to develop a park system plan, with boulevards, in addition to his regular duties as superintendent.

Schwagerl presented his plan just a few months later, in September 1892, to a meeting of businessmen at the Chamber of Commerce. *The Seattle Post-*

Intelligencer listed the prominent community members who attended the meeting, including park board chairman Daniel Jones, property owner David Denny, his son John B. Denny, business and civic leader Thomas Prosch, developer George Kinnear, and architect Charles W. Saunders (who would later be deeply involved in the Board of Park Commissioners and work closely with Olmsted and his associates).

According to the *Seattle Post-Intelligencer*'s account of the meeting, Schwagerl's presentation began with a summary of why parks were needed in a city, followed by a description of how Seattle's abundant natural beauty made it well-situated for parks. Schwagerl reiterated the need to plan for the future and acquire real estate before it was developed or became too expensive. He shared a map marked with four sites for large parks: one to the northeast of the city, on Lake Washington (today's Magnuson Park), a second in the southeast, on a peninsula extending into the lake (later the site of Seward Park), a third in the southwest, at Alki Point, and a fourth to the northwest, at West Point (later the site of Fort Lawton, then Discovery Park). He called for a lakeshore boulevard to connect the parks on the eastern side of the city and other boulevards, or "attenuated parks" as he called them, echoing Frederick Law Olmsted Sr.'s terminology. The *Seattle Post-Intelligencer* reporter described the boulevards as "simply avenues so built and planted with trees and grass plats as to convey to those walking on them the impression of being in a park." Schwagerl estimated

Seattle, looking east from the King Street coal bunker, 1882.

Seattle waterfront looking north from about Washington Street, 1887.

a cost of $10 million or more (about $280 million in 2019 dollars) to fully realize his vision, but the immediate cost to acquire the land and determine the routes of boulevards so they could be incorporated into plats would be much less. He explained that the remaining costs to develop the parks and boulevards could be spread out over 20 years.

The plan seems to have been received favorably by the meeting's attendees. Banker and Chamber of Commerce president Edward O. Graves made a motion that it be approved, "in a general way" and that the city council require all future subdivision plats to conform to it. Mayor James T. Ronald announced to those assembled that the city government fully supported Schwagerl's plan. A committee was then formed to promote public support of it. This practice of policy-making by influential civic leaders was common at that time. Property owners—largely male, white, and middle class—would have assumed that they should decide what land to reserve for parks and boulevards. Seattle was a frontier city, where people took significant risks investing in the emerging economy, and economic growth became its raison d'être—with all efforts focused on attracting further investment and settlement. It would later be necessary to get voters (at that time, all male citizens who could speak and read English) citywide to approve bonds to acquire land, but others who had an interest in land use or park distribution but did not have the right to vote, such as women or Native people, were not brought into the planning process.

Although Schwagerl's plan was well received, Seattle saw little progress in park development in the 1890s. In addition to some improvements to Lake View Park on Capitol Hill (Washelli Cemetery had been converted into a park in 1887), Kinnear Park was donated in 1887 by George and Angie Kinnear, prominent residents of Queen Anne Hill. The city acquired Woodland Park in 1899 from the Guy Phinney Estate and his widow, Nellie Phinney, and a large part of what would become Washington Park in January 1900. Three small squares, Pioneer Place, Fortson Place, both downtown, and Howard Place, off Eastlake Avenue East, were set aside and improved for public use.

The delay in realizing Schwagerl's plan was largely due to the country falling into an economic tailspin as the Panic of 1893 wiped out investments and caused economic stagnation. In Seattle, 11 banks failed in the first year and property values dropped by up to 80 percent. City growth ground to a near halt, with just 35 plats filed in King County between May 1893 and 1897, compared to 395 in the three years prior to the crash.

Other factors conspired to hold back the plan. Regrading projects and sewer and water system development drew attention (and money) away from park development. The Board of Park Commissioners proved ineffectual in pushing any projects forward. And, as Schwagerl explained in 1894, "Notwithstanding the apparent indifference evinced by some in regard to the devising of some system of continuous driveways around the city at the

Path in Woodland Park, 1904.

SEATTLE
"The Queen City"
KLONDIKE — ALASKA

SEATTLE, "The Queen City of the Northwest, founded in 1852, the Commercial, Manufacturing, Railroad, Mining, and Agricultural Centre of Washington State, has," according to *Harper's Weekly*, "practically monopolized the Alaskan outfitting business." The reason is that Seattle, 65,000 population, is the largest city in the Pacific Northwest. Look at the map! With three transcontinental railroads to any other city's one, producing her own flour, woollens, hardware, and other articles of miners' outfits, she has keener mercantile competition and lower prices than elsewhere. Canadian customs are a bugbear. Much of a miner's outfit goes in free. 70 per cent. of a Canadian outfit is American made. Seattle has outfitted more men and sent more vessels north than all other ports. She is ready for all. Her harbor is perfect, climate superb, death rate the lowest, people most progressive, commerce growing, manufactures flourishing. Volume of business in '96 was $15,282,000. Steamship lines to Alaska, Japan, Central America. $5,500,000 manufactures. Great Federal improvements under way. State of Washington is best in United States for agricultural settlers. Wheat crop nearly 25,000,000 bushels. Cereals, fruits, hops, coal, and minerals are the source of great wealth. Every steamship line but one leaves Seattle. You must go there before you can get to Alaska. Do not be deceived by misleading or false statements to the contrary.

Look at your map! Seattle is a commercial city, and is to the Pacific Northwest as New York is to the Atlantic coast. All railroads in United States connect with three great transcontinental lines running to Seattle.

For Free Information address

Information Bureau

CHAMBER OF COMMERCE
SEATTLE, WASHINGTON, U. S.

Seattle's Chamber of Commerce actively promoted the city as the "Queen City" of the Pacific Northwest and the ideal launching point for the gold fields of Alaska and the Klondike River in Canada's Yukon Territory.

earliest possible date, a large number of intelligent property owners and sound business men continue quietly to agitate the subject, though the general plans proposed during the past two years have proved to be so comprehensive and vast in extent to render a commencement along these lines too difficult for the present." Schwagerl left his position in 1895, having accomplished little more than implementing his designs for Denny and Kinnear Parks.

The most substantive work on recreational facilities in the city would actually be carried out by the Queen City Good Roads Club. In response to the surge in bicycling in the city, the club began building bicycle paths in 1897, receiving permission from the city to run their eight-foot paths in street rights-of-way. George Cotterill got involved in early 1898, becoming the chair of the club's path committee. He provided a significant benefit to the project because of his professional role as assistant city engineer. The paths passed through city parks, provided connections between them, and followed the shorelines of Lake Union and Lake Washington.

Had a strong park superintendent gotten established, he might have been able to move the park plan forward, but absent that leadership, the Board of Park Commissioners fell into squabbling and disinterest in the 1890s. Most of the commissioners appear to have done very little and attended few meetings. By April 1897, things had devolved substantially. Park commissioner C. D. C. Williams handwrote an annual park report to the city council

and warned that Schwagerl's "Million Dollar Boulevard is a Myth [and] the sooner this is attended to the better, before the Park funds are cut off." He ended his screed with a zinger about the state of City Park (Volunteer Park): "You might as well expect to raise an Electric Plant in the City park by planting Electric Bulbs, as to grow Roses therein and have them a success."

Even with the turnaround in Seattle's economy after the start of the Klondike Gold Rush in July 1897, little changed with the Board of Park Commissioners. A new city charter adopted in 1896 reorganized the park board, reduced them to advisors, and delegated control of the park fund and the parks to the city council. In 1901, Williams and Melody Choir, the only other active commissioner, delivered dueling annual reports to the city council. Choir filed what must be the most distinctive annual report in the city archives. In it, he railed against the ineffectiveness of the Board of Park Commissioners and offered a summary of desirable commissioner qualifications, one of which was "possessed of sufficient wealth to merit the respect and esteem of men-of-affairs." He called for a reinstatement of the salary for commissioners, which had been cut during the economic depression, a badge (but not a brass one), and no more than three commissioners on the board. He also offered to do all of the commission's work for $2,000 annually. Choir ended with an elaborate scheme for a comfort station at Pioneer Place, saltwater beaches with heated water to encourage

Two women on a bike path along Lake Union, ca. 1901. This cinder-covered trail began at 8th Avenue and Pine Street and passed through the woods to Lake Washington via what would later be the routes of Lakeview and Interlaken Boulevards.

First page of park commissioner Melody Choir's 1901 report to the city council.

"random romps and sportive dives," and small parks distributed throughout the city, not the large, somewhat remote ones recommended by Schwagerl.

C. D. C. Williams' dour report contrasted sharply with Choir's colorful and expansive submission. He warned against allowing streetcars in parks because of the potential for accidents (he beseeched them to "picture the mother carrying the mangled form of her little one Home from a days outing at Wood Land Park") and complained of not being able to compete with Choir because of his ability to offer banquets at his home for city council members, a thinly veiled jab at the council's corruptibility.

The Board of Park Commissioners continued to spin its wheels into 1902. Williams resigned in March because Mayor Thomas J. Humes insisted on referring to him as a committee member, not a commissioner, and would not give him a free streetcar pass. Humes may have been forgiven for the kerfuffle with Williams, but fault for the failure in appointing two other candidates to the board lies with him. In 1902, he nominated John F. Cragwell, an African American barbershop owner, to the board. Confirmation of Cragwell's appointment became contentious when some members of the local black community objected that he was not deserving because he had not actually supported Humes in the recent election. There appears to be more to the story than party politics. According to historian Quintard Taylor in *The Forging of a Black Community*, Cragwell refused to serve black customers in his barber shops in order to avoid driving away white customers, a dilemma created by the discriminatory climate of the day. To resolve the park board problem, Humes appointed a second African American commissioner, Richard Davis. This did not appease Cragwell's opponents, and neither Cragwell nor Davis took their seats on the board.

Several aspects of the Cragwell-Davis incident illustrate why the board was ineffective in this period. First, the appointment of park commissioners was highly politicized and linked with patronage. Further, given that Cragwell and Davis were the only black commissioners considered in this era, the black community was clearly not represented on the board even though extensive coverage of park issues in the city's African American newspaper, *The Seattle Republican*, indicates wide interest in parks within the black community. *The Seattle Times* professed in an editorial that it did not object to African American commissioners per se, but questioned Cragwell's and Davis' proficiency in park work. This disclaimer rings hollow given that other park commissioners, for the most part, appear to have had only prominence in civic matters to recommend them for service on the park board. Finally, the fact that other park board appointments floundered shows that instead of being seen as patronage, it was a political favor to the mayor to serve for no pay and with no real power.

With the Board of Park Commissioners largely ineffective, the park system also ran up against commercial interests regarding land use. State legislator Andrew Hemrich introduced a bill in 1901 to grant lands exposed by the anticipated lowering of Lake Washington after construction of the ship canal to the City of Seattle for a park boulevard. Seattle lawyer and civic leader John J. McGilvra wrote a letter to *The Seattle Times* claiming:

> *This so called boulevard scheme seems to be a sort of mania that occasionally affects the brainless promoters of wild and visionary schemes. . . . This monstrosity would destroy or greatly damage every home there is or is to be on the Lake shore, and greatly interfere with wharves, warehouses, shipping and commerce generally . . . shores will be devoted to trade and commerce, not to fancy boulevards.*

McGilvra was deeply involved in efforts to build the Lake Washington Ship Canal, the primary purpose of which was to open up the city's freshwater shorelines for industrial development. In the face of direct competition with business interests, the park boulevard bill failed.

In the absence of park board leadership, business leaders attempted to jump-start park system development. The Chamber of Commerce convened a meeting in February 1902 to discuss how they should proceed. Edward Schwagerl, then in private practice as a landscape architect, presented his 1892 plan. It was again well-received, and those present called for the reorganization of the Board of Park Commissioners, giving it the power to acquire land and to manage the Park Department. Park superintendent Frank Little, who was a member of the Board of Public Works, a board with actual power, attended the meeting. It appears that he soon began to work behind the scenes to promote the park plan.

John J. McGilvra's Eagle Baths, boathouse, and dance pavilion at Madison Park, ca. 1901.

Photo of Lake Washington shoreline taken by Percy Jones in May 1903.

While the exact sequence of events has been lost to time, at some point after the Chamber meeting, Little talked with James D. Blackwell, a Seattle Electric Company engineer, about how the company's streetcar should be routed through Woodland Park in its circuit around Green Lake. This issue had caused consternation because of concerns about bisecting the park and the streetcar traffic's impact on the park experience. The next month, Blackwell wrote to Percy Jones, an associate in the Olmsted Brothers firm. Blackwell referenced Superintendent Little in his letter, implying that they had discussed reaching out to the Olmsted firm. Blackwell inquired whether "Mr. Olmstead" would be available to plan the area of Woodland Park jointly owned by the city and the Seattle Electric Company. He was concerned that the landscaping in the right-of-way would be "butchered by persons unskilled in park work if left in local hands." He was looking for advice from Olmsted or "some good landscape architect," and wondering if they would recommend a "Mr. Kelsie [Kelsey], from Boston," who was expected to arrive in Seattle soon. Beyond the firm's national reputation, it is not clear why Blackwell directed the inquiry to the Olmsted Brothers. It is likely that he remembered the firm from his years working in Boston for the Boston and Albany Railroad Company and for the City of Boston Board of Survey.

Jones sent Blackwell's letter along to John Olmsted, asking if he would like to reply. A couple of days later, Olmsted sent a letter to Blackwell. He began with some hesitancy because of the distance involved and recommended a visit of several days, which would allow a landscape architect to prepare a general plan and a report. He quoted a price of $5,000 plus travel expenses and ended with a note that "the preparation of such a topographical plan even on the reduced terms which we have named would involve so large an expenditure that it seems hardly probable that the [Seattle] Park Commission and City Government would agree to it. If you conclude that such is the case we have no doubt we can help you to some cheaper professional assistance." Olmsted could not, however, recommend Mr. Kelsey, citing the failure of his nursery business.

A month later, after consulting with Superintendent Little and the Board of Park Commissioners, Blackwell reported to the Olmsted Brothers that Little had succeeded in raising interest in hiring the firm and mentioned a map of Seattle that he would be sending along to give them a sense of the city. He didn't explicitly say so, but the interest appears to have shifted to having the firm consult on the entire park system, not just Woodland Park. Not incidentally, at about this time, in April 1902, the Reverend Thomas L. Eliot, a member of the Portland Board of Park Commissioners, wrote to Little about their plan to hire the Olmsted Brothers to develop a citywide park system plan. Eliot shared some of the letters between the Olmsted Brothers and the Portland commissioners with Little.

This may have been the spark that got the Board of Park Commissioners on track to hire the Olmsted Brothers. Seattleites had long competed with Portland for the title of Queen City of the Pacific Northwest, and the idea that their rival might be first to get a park and boulevard system designed by an East Coast expert would likely have spurred them to action.

Propelled by the competition and the possibility of bringing an Olmsted to Seattle, civic leaders began in earnest to push forward the effort to develop a park system. By July a new park board had been appointed. The new president, Elbert F. Blaine, was a prominent lawyer. The other members were architect Charles W. Saunders, civil engineer Charles E. Fowler, business owner J. Edward Shrewsbury, and wealthy "eccentric" Melody Choir, the only holdover from the old board. While the new park board did not yet have any real power, it had a fresh slate of men with financial interests in seeing the park system developed and with the social and economic standing to realize their goals.

The city also had a handful of park properties in need of development. City residents wanted to see paths, drives, and flower beds in Woodland and Volunteer Parks, and something other than a dusty empty lot adjacent to Lincoln Reservoir. Through the summer and fall of 1902, the board carried out tours of inspection and attempted to persuade Seattleites to support a levy or an increased budget allocation for park acquisition. The park commissioners sent a letter to "principal taxpayers" in the city asking if they would support a levy to fund the development of a park system. The newspapers reported that they received a positive response. In late September, the *Seattle Post-Intelligencer* ran a full-page article titled " 'Let Us Make a Beautiful City of Seattle,' Say the Park Commissioners." It made multiple arguments for why the city needed a park system, quoting

BOARD OF PARK COMMISSIONERS

E. F. BLAINE — CHAIRMAN

CHARLES W. SAUNDERS — SECRETARY

The City of Seattle Washington

E. F. BLAINE
C. E. FOWLER
J. E. SHREWSBURY
M. CHOIR
C. W. SAUNDERS
COMMISSIONERS

Dear Sir: From the good old town of Springfield, Massachusetts, we have borrowed the motto "Let us make a beautiful city of" Seattle. The task is not an easy one. To accomplish it there must be co-operation and a strong public sentiment. The sorid grasp for money, and intense commercialism of some of our citizens, must give way to saner ideas.

The first fact that must be admitted is that Seattle, from an artistic point of view, is behind every city of her size in the United States. There is not, except in name, a foot of boulevard within her corporate limits. Our improved parks are but large squares; they are three in number--Denny, Kinnear and Volunteer. Woodland Park except the wooded portion, for lack of water is brown and uninviting. The truth is, when a friend visits us from abroad, we are ashamed to mention our parks. Every time a delegation, congressional or otherwise, visits our city we strive to divert their thoughts from the barrenness of the immediate scene to the beautiful panorama of lakes, sound, mountains and peaks beyond. This city, except in her business section, in ragged and haphazard. Not a hundredth part of the land platted has been laid off with reference to the topography of the ground. Every day's delay makes more difficult the problem of parks and boulevards. At the present time trees within the city are being felled for cordwood, which if preserved in a park would have a value and a charm incalculable.

Seattle can be made beautiful. Her scenery is unsurpassed. Give her local charm and she will become famous as a residential city. Parks and boulevards are the essentials. They will prove here as they have proven everywhere, incentives to artistic development.

Every city of importance in our country is alive to the merits of esthetic development.

The Metropolitan Park system in and about Boston is to cost $10,000,000. St. Paul in 1901, spent on her parks and boulevards $128,284; Minneapolis, $203,921; Detroit, $145,265; Kansas City, $132,500; Denver, $91,466; San Francisco, $255,362; Los Angeles, $65,221; Seattle, $10,685. These figures ought to be humiliating to our pride. The lack of taste and indifference paid to our parks and drives is abominable. We offer no criticism of public officers as no money worth mentioning has been spent.

We want your opinion as to what ought to be done, and done now as the tax levy is about to be made.

In Minneapolis the levy for parks and boulevards is one mill. In Cambridge, Massachusetts, the tax for parks and boulevards per capita in 1901 was 96c; Hartford, 88c; Los Angeles, 64c; San Francisco, 70c; Denver, 57c; Kansas City, 84c. There can be no question but that Seattle has 100,000 people. Can she not, ought she not in 1903 to expend at least $60,000 or 60c per capita for parks or boulevards?

An immediate answer will be appreciated.

Yours respectfully,

Geo. F. Cotterill

E. Blaine
C. E. Fowler
M. Choir
C. W. Saunders
Ed Shrewsbury

Sept. 5, '02.

Board of Park Commissioners letter sent to influential Seattleites in September 1902 to enlist their support for a park system.

city council members, former park superintendent Schwagerl, and many prominent city residents. It also repeatedly pointed to the strides made in other cities to develop park systems. Despite this and other indications that Seattle residents supported the park commissioners' vision, neither the levy nor the budget increase came to pass that fall.

In December 1902, park board secretary Charles Saunders wrote to Frederick Law Olmsted Jr. directly. He probably sought out Rick because he shared a name with his well-known father and because Saunders had been exchanging letters with the Portland Board of Park Commissioners, which had also been corresponding with the younger Olmsted. Saunders explained that they were seeking someone

to advise us in the proper laying out of a system by which we can not only improve the land owned by us for park purposes, situated in the different portions of the city, but also to devise a series of roadways and parkways which will tie these isolated tracts together, as well as suggest an improvement of the squares and open places under our control.

He sweetened the deal by suggesting that the University of Washington Board of Regents would also hire the firm to design a plan for the university's campus if the state legislature appropriated funding for it in 1903.

Saunders sent along a map of the city and some other informational pamphlets, but did not mention the Schwagerl plan. He asked what the terms would be for such a project and ended with the observation,

We feel sure that the problem of improvements of the parks of our city will prove a very interesting one to you, for it possesses not only a peculiar and varied

30

"Let Us Make a Beautiful City of Seattle," Say the Park Commissioners

Seattle Post-Intelligencer *article announcing the Board of Park Commissioners plan to develop a park system, September 21, 1902.*

contour, but it is also rich in natural scenery of
mountains, lakes and sound, and the opportunities
for a Park System are certainly far beyond the average
of other cities throughout the United States.

John Olmsted responded promptly with two letters, each signed "Olmsted Brothers." One outlined the terms under which he would do the project. It described how he and an assistant would look over the landscape for one to two weeks and then prepare a report and a map locating the parks and parkways. The firm would also provide advice over the course of 1903. He did not mention anything about more extensive plans for individual landscapes. The total charge would be $1,000 plus traveling and other expenses, and he enclosed a circular describing their process.

The other letter was a more informal communication. Olmsted relayed the terms that could be worked out if Portland also hired the Olmsted Brothers. It would reduce the cost to $850 because of the more efficient use of the time spent traveling to the Pacific Northwest. The letter explained that Rick Olmsted would be available in the summer, after he finished teaching at Harvard for the year, or John Olmsted, the senior partner, would be available within a week or two of notification that Seattle would like to proceed with the firm. The letter included a list of parks Olmsted had been professionally connected with, to help inform the park commissioners of the firm's experience and prominence. In particular, the letter called out the work John Olmsted had recently done with the Essex County park system in New Jersey.

It is interesting to look at the difference in the terms between the earlier communication about Woodland Park, when they asked for $5,000 for work on one park design, and the later one, when the firm quoted $850 for a report for an entire system plan. Part of the difference may have been the anticipated scope of work. For a park design project, they may have assumed there would be numerous studies and plans for grading, circulation, planting, and other technical aspects. It is possible, however, that the inquiry from Portland shifted the terms in more than just the travel expenses. Prior to these projects, the only work the firm had done on the West Coast was in California. The Pacific Northwest would be a new expansion, adding more travel on top of their already-extensive reach into the South and Midwest. John Olmsted regularly made circuits between job locations in Ohio, Georgia, Illinois, and Missouri. He also traveled often around New England. His brother had recently completed his work in Washington, D.C., on preparation of the McMillan Plan.

To some extent they could work while traveling on trains, although John's personal letters to his wife, Sophie, often included complaints about how much time was lost in travel and the difficulty of writing reports while on the move. Despite these frustrations, Olmsted had raised traveling by train to an art. He could rattle off train schedules in letters with the same facility that the most seasoned public transportation

The Knickerbocker

Allan A. Wright · Proprietor

Seattle, 4th May 1903

My Dear Wife;

You do not seem quite so far away as I received your letter of 30th April when I got to the hotel about 6.45 this evening. But part of this apparent shortness in the time may have been due to your having dated your letter a day ahead. At any rate it is postmarked Boston 29th – 8 P.M.

I am sorry your new nurse seemed so likely to disappoint you.

I am alarmed by your saying you might send one more letter here. I thought I had put on my memorandum of address the time I should be here as 2 weeks. I am under agreement to stay that long so I knew it before I left. As a matter of fact I am almost certain to be here 3 weeks and I may stay longer. So I hope you will continue writing me until I notify you of date of leaving here & give my next address.

One of John Olmsted's nearly daily letters to his wife, Sophie Olmsted, written on Knickerbocker Hotel stationery. Olmsted also stayed at the Rainier Club several times during his visits to Seattle.

Captain John F. Pratt

Captain John F. Pratt began his service with the U.S. Coast and Geodetic Survey upon graduating from Dartmouth College in 1871. The Coast and Geodetic Survey (now the National Geodetic Survey) was responsible for surveying the American coast and creating nautical charts to be used by ships as they negotiated their way through coastal waters. He came to the Northwest in 1884 to work along the Washington and Alaska coasts. He also led one of the parties that surveyed the Alaskan boundary with Canada and helped locate the Puget Sound Naval Shipyard at Bremerton. After several years working off the coasts of California, Alaska, and the Hawaiian Islands, he would be placed in command of the survey ship *Pathfinder* from 1908 until 1912. From 1912 until his retirement in 1920, Captain Pratt was at the head of the Seattle field station. He stayed in Seattle after his retirement, until his death in 1929.

Captain John Pratt, seated in front row, center, on the U.S. Coast and Geodetic Survey ship Pathfinder *in 1903.*

user might discuss a city's bus routes. He provided Sophie with a list of hotels and the dates on which she should address her letters to each one. They kept up a daily correspondence and regularly compared notes on the transit times of their letters, carefully comparing postmark dates *and* times to assess the speed of their delivery. In this way, he was able to keep in close contact with his family despite his long absences and often-missed holidays.

In mid-January 1903, Saunders replied to the Olmsted Brothers on behalf of the Board of Park Commissioners, emphasizing their desire to have a comprehensive system and their understanding that although the University of Washington job was separate, that project and others for private clients in Tacoma and Seattle would likely be forthcoming. The Olmsted Brothers replied that Rick could come if Seattle was willing to wait until summer, but the contract would be signed with the firm, implying that Seattle's project would be handled by whoever was available when it began. After negotiations via telegrams and telephone calls to Portland to try to coordinate their plans, the contract was finally signed between the Board of Public Works and the Olmsted Brothers on February 28, 1903.

Just before the contract was signed, the city hired United States Coast and Geodetic Survey Captain John F. Pratt to compile the data gathered and the surveys prepared for the park system project. Pratt traveled to Washington, D.C., for official business in March 1903 and carried several maps with him. He met with John Olmsted on March 19 to show him the maps and discuss the Seattle project. Although much of the rhetoric of the public park movement focused on providing access to parks for all classes, there was also a distinct middle- and upper-class real estate development element to their discussion of park planning in Seattle. Olmsted summarized the information Pratt provided in his meeting notes, writing,

> The better class of people are mostly young, married and have families, so the school population is unusually large and as these people have all their money in their business they rent their house and have no horses and carriages. Hence, the first developments should be in the existing parks which have electric car communication, in order to popularize the parks and win opinion with more liberal park expenditures.

He further noted, "He [Pratt] said nothing about additional parks large or small and I inferred that the main effort at present would be to get parkways as these would, some of them [,] benefit real estate schemes."

And with that, John Olmsted's work in Seattle began.

JOHN CHARLES OLMSTED.   FREDERICK LAW OLMSTED, JR.

OLMSTED BROTHERS.
LANDSCAPE ARCHITECTS.

BROOKLINE, MASS.

24th December, 1902.

Mr. Charles W. Saunders, Secretary,

Board of Park Commissioners,

Seattle, Washington,

Dear Sir:-

We have the honor to acknowledge your letter of the 16th instant and to submit herein, as requested, our proposition for a preliminary visit and report.

As we have already submitted a proposition with regard to a general plan for Woodland Park and the property of the Seattle Electric Company adjoining it we shall confine the present proposition to what we are accustomed to call a preliminary visit and report with regard to a general system of proposed parks and parkways.

A member of our firm will make a visit to Seattle within a short time after we are notified that your Commission is ready to receive him. He will spend what time he finds to be necessary, presumably at least a week and more probably nearer a fortnight, in examining the city and the surrounding

ssioners and

ced assistants

and will

t as may be

Mr. Olmsted

ort accom-

ict considered,

approximate

ays. We

l plan

ve can

spondence

location

s as we

isit,

prove to

to defi-

ld expect

s long as

tional

uld be

d for

depen-

visit and

ned will be one thousand dollars

s for services of assistants and

including subsistence while away

ental expenses, as explained in

nted circular which we make a part

Yours very truly,

Olmsted Brothers

E.F.

Letter from the Olmsted Brothers to Charles Saunders, sent December 24, 1902, outlining the terms under which they would develop a park system plan for Seattle.

[enclosure with
24th December 1902.]

JOHN CHARLES OLMSTED.   FREDERICK LAW OLMSTED, JR.

OLMSTED BROTHERS,

LANDSCAPE ARCHITECTS.

BROOKLINE, MASS.

STATEMENT AS TO PROFESSIONAL METHODS AND CHARGES.

Our business is the supplying of professional advice with respect to the arrangement of land for use, and the accompanying landscape for enjoyment. We design or revise the arrangement of private grounds and gardens, public parks and squares, suburban neighborhoods, town sites, streets, and parkways. We consult with owners, architects, engineers, and gardeners concerning the placing of buildings, the laying out of roads, the grading of surfaces, and the treatment of new or old plantations. In general we advise as to the arrangement of land and the objects upon it for any purpose whatsoever where the appearance of the result is worth consideration.

PRELIMINARY VISIT.

The first step in our employment is a preliminary visit to the ground and a consultation with the client. This visit binds neither party to any further dealings with the other. Verbal suggestions of considerable value can often be made on the spot; while if plans, designs, or written reports are called for, the preliminary visit enables us to acquire much of the general information upon which these can be based. When it appears that a topographical map is needed for the proper study of the problem, instructions as to the making of the survey are prepared by us without extra charge. We ourselves are not surveyors. If the client knows in advance that he desires from us a design drawn to a scale, the necessary surveyor's map should be made ready for our use on the occasion of our first visit.

PRELIMINARY AND GENERAL PLANS.

Upon the basis of the topographical map we design a preliminary plan embodying the ideas suggested at the preliminary visit, with such other ideas as closer study or additional visits may have evolved. The preliminary plan is intended to be examined, criticised, and discussed, in order that a better solution of the given problem may, if possible, be reached. If changes prove to be desirable, a revised preliminary plan is prepared. In case the problem is concerned with any buildings, our preliminary plan should be made in advance of the building plans, and our subsequent drawings should include the results of consultations with the architect of the buildings.

constructive emergencies, to order necessary changes, and to define the true intent and meaning of the drawings and specifications, and he has authority to stop the progress of the work and order its removal when not in accordance with them."

subsequent stage until we ...

BROOKLINE, MASS., January 1st, 1902.

---

have been approved, the next step is ...ble constructions, the controling figures ...re important modifications of existing ...ortant cases by an explanatory report, ...lements of the design which might not ...plan, or a revision of it, serves as a ...ssessed of suitable technical training, ...ut occasional visits and more or less

...RVISION.

...n of our general plans to their own ...we are always prepared to make ...ervise days' work or contract work, ...ositions, shapes, and sizes of every ...The specifications describe what- ...quality of materials and the kind ...procuring of bids from reliable ...ork as contractors, nor do we act ...ontract or by the day, our practice ...ary responsibility for the qualities ...re made primarily with reference ...ct as a check on the contractor, ...de in them have been examined ...upervision of a competent resident

...ION.

...of such parts of our general plans ...ays ready to advise our clients ...changes in existing vegetation, ...y planting. When asked to do ...is are approved, it is our custom ...nts. We are systematically at ...carrying out of planting plans ...we are able to secure plants at

...rchitects :—
continuous personal superintendence ...ion by the architect, or his deputy, of ...ds necessary to ascertain whether

---

...e advantage. We are not gardeners, nor are we ...rchases. We are not responsible for errors of ...ts in transportation, or for their failure to grow. ...e are accustomed to direct such gardeners or ...rpretation to be put upon our plans, and the best ...rchitects do in the case of buildings. ...ed and executed, they need to be intelligently ...e always glad to advise our clients year after year ...ants to attend to the details of such work.

...ES.

...i desired, be agreed upon in advance) is ordinarily ...nding upon the importance and difficulty of the ...ot expected that we should report in writing. The ...ur assistants are always to be refunded to us by our ...the course of a tour, these expenses are divided. ...l, our charge is generally made up of a professional ...$50.00 for a small building lot to some thousands

...special disbursements by us required in connection ..., telegrams, expressage, sunprints, photographs, and ...ting all plans made in our office, collecting needed ..., estimating, selecting, and ordering plants, visiting ...ll we may have done for the client by means of our ...l services, for which we are paid by the professional ...with our assistants' services are of a general nature ...l clients without an extravagantly elaborate system ...he actual amounts paid to assistants for the hours ...k of each client.

...and other needed information furnished us free of ...gs, which remain in our possession, and from which ...y be needed by our clients and the engineers, archi- ...be concerned.

...fications, and supervision of construction, we charge a ...gning and supervision, plus expenses.

...and ordering plants and supervision of planting, we

...e charge a comparatively small annual professional fee,

...e Preliminary Visit, the Preliminary and General Plans, ...lanting Plans, and we do not usually proceed to any ...o.

The Olmsted Brothers sent this "Statement as to Professional Methods and Charges" to prospective clients.

36

Contour map with red line given to John Olmsted in March 1903 when he met with Captain Pratt in Washington, D.C., before coming to Seattle. It appears Olmsted made additional handwritten notes on the plan.

John Olmsted at the drafting table at Fairsted, the Olmsted family home and the Olmsted Brothers' office.

CHAPTER 2
WHAT IS "OLMSTEDIAN"?

When John Olmsted received word in early March 1903 that he might be needed in Seattle and so might not have a chance to go home to Brookline, Massachusetts, before heading west, he wrote to his wife, Sophie, "I fear this means that I shall have to go right out there. It would be quite a surprise if I should have to go right along from Pittsburgh or Atlanta without even getting home. . . . I would rather Rick would go this summer. I don't want to be so long gone from my wife and home." Given the enormous distance between Brookline and Seattle, more than 3,000 miles, why did Seattle decide to incur the expense, inconvenience, and risk of hiring someone largely unknown to Seattleites?

First and foremost, the Olmsted reputation preceded him. Frederick Law Olmsted's work on Central Park and the World's Columbian Exposition in Chicago was celebrated across the country. For nearly 50 years, city governments had been hiring the Olmsted firms in their various permutations from Olmsted & Vaux to Olmsted Brothers, Landscape Architects. John Charles Olmsted had joined his stepfather's firm in 1875, after graduating from Yale. He worked with him on a number of projects, including the Back Bay Fens in Boston and Biltmore in North Carolina, before the elder Olmsted retired. Then, as a senior partner in the Olmsted Brothers firm, John led the Essex County, Atlanta, Louisville, and Chicago park system projects. He also worked on plans for the New York state capitol grounds in Albany, the Cornell College campus in Iowa, and the plan for Stanford University. Just prior to arriving in Seattle, he was working on a landscape plan for a Catalina Island resort in Southern California.

Hiring the Olmsted Brothers firm provided validation for the park system project in the public

The view across Lake Washington to Mount Rainier captures Olmsted's use of borrowed landscape in locating Lake Washington Boulevard along the lakeshore.

The name Olmsted is synonymous with landscape architecture, but it is not generally understood that it represents two generations of a family who helped shape the field and the American landscape. The elder Frederick Law Olmsted is commonly referred to as "Senior" today, to differentiate him from the younger Frederick Law Olmsted, his son, who was known as "Rick" to family members and colleagues. Neither man regularly referred to himself as Senior or Junior, leading to significant confusion over the years about who did what and when. Likewise, there were several John Olmsteds in the family tree, but each had a different middle name. Seattle's Olmsted was John Charles Olmsted. He often signed his own name as either John C. Olmsted or J. C. Olmsted, but is most commonly referred to as simply John Olmsted in correspondence. To keep the family members straight in this book, we have chosen to refer to the elder Olmsted as Frederick Law Olmsted Sr., the younger as Rick, and John Charles Olmsted as John Olmsted.

Portrait of John Charles and Sophia White Olmsted.

mind. Newspaper accounts reference Olmsted's connection to Boston, his expertise, and his family connections. By bringing him to Seattle, the commissioners drew a connection between the work they wanted to do and the East Coast standard for park planning. It helped justify such a large undertaking to have that stamp of legitimacy.

Perhaps unknown to the Board of Park Commissioners, however, they also gained access to a body of experience and deep knowledge of design principles that formed the foundation of landscape architecture in the United States. The Olmsted firms had largely defined the field of landscape architecture.

Rick helped establish the landscape architecture program at Harvard University, the first such program in the country. The brothers helped found the American Society of Landscape Architects in 1899, with John serving as the organization's first president. Through their work, they pioneered principles that are still fundamental to the landscape architecture and planning professions.

In approaching a site, whether a park, a boulevard, a university campus, or a private residence, John Olmsted looked first at what made it unique. He then built the design around that "genius of place," taking into account the views, the existing vegetation, the surroundings, and the site's relationship to other places. An excellent example of this in Seattle is Rainier Vista, on the University of Washington campus. That view corridor served as an axis of the world's fair grounds in 1909. The view framed by evergreen trees draws the eye across Lake Washington to the forested foothills and then to the magnificence

Cherokee Park, part of the Olmsted-designed Louisville Park system.

Waterway in the Back Bay Fens, Boston.

Adapted from the National Association for Olmsted Parks' "Chronology of the Olmsted Firm 1857–1979."

of Mount Rainier. It brings a view that is unique to the city and, actually, unique to that one place, into the heart of the campus. Throughout the city, Olmsted incorporated views across waterways to mountains into designs for parks and boulevards in a practice often referred to as "borrowed landscape." Likewise, the park system as a whole was organized to take advantage of the particular natural beauty of the city, with parks on hilltops and hillsides and boulevards in forested ravines and along shorelines.

An Olmsted design encompasses an entire landscape. The paths and drives, open areas and thickly vegetated areas, viewpoints looking into or outward from the landscape, water features, structures, buildings, and activities are arranged so they come together in a unified composition. For West Seattle's Hiawatha Playfield design, Olmsted laid out spaces for team sports, playground equipment, a fieldhouse, gymnastic apparatus, and landscape features such as groves of trees and planting beds, with attention paid to the needs of each area's intended users. Paths wrap around the perimeter from each of the pedestrian entries and connect with other paths leading to the fieldhouse. The park has been

Olmsted Park System Design Principles

When John Olmsted developed a park system for a city, he was guided by a number of overarching design principles:

GENERAL DESIGN

- Respond to local environment and topography
- Retain the local landscape character
- Take advantage of views, particularly of water and mountains
- Incorporate existing water features
- Subordinate built structures to the landscape and its features

FOR PARKS

- Include a range of park sizes to serve different purposes and meet a range of needs
- Distribute parks throughout the city to provide access for all residents
- Provide a variety of designs so each park is different from others in the system
- Incorporate spaces for active and passive recreation throughout the system

FOR PARKWAYS & BOULEVARDS

- Use parkways and boulevards as links between parks so that they form a cohesive system
- Locate parkways and boulevards so that they provide access from all parts of the city to parks and landscape features
- Provide sufficient width to allow the landscape to be a feature of the parkway or boulevard experience
- Incorporate additional parkland adjacent to parkways and boulevards, where conditions allow

altered over time, but the same graceful balance of landscape and sports facilities remains.

Olmsted paid particular attention to circulation routes and the allotment of space for activities. In contrast to city sidewalks, where, as Olmsted Sr. said, "those conditions . . . compel us to walk circumspectly, watchfully, jealously, which compel us to look upon others without sympathy," park paths were separated from drives by vegetation and lawns, or located on different grades, allowing for contemplative and carefree movement through the park. As much as possible, these paths and drives conformed to the topography (whether natural or regraded), and curved and meandered across landscapes. This obscured the end point of a path or drive, giving the impression of indefinite length, and provided a sense of being immersed in the landscape. The concourse drive in Volunteer Park curves along the ridge so its end points are not visible from one end

Richardson Bridge over the Muddy River in the Back Bay Fens, Boston.

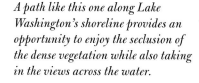

On the Shore of Lake Washington, Seattle, Wash.

A path like this one along Lake Washington's shoreline provides an opportunity to enjoy the seclusion of the dense vegetation while also taking in the views across the water.

Rainier Vista at the University of Washington.

to the other, giving the feeling of a much longer drive than its 945 feet.

Olmsted balanced and organized space for specific activities, such as ballfields or playgrounds, with contemplative spaces such as overlooks, lawns, or water features. This balance extended beyond individual parks into the park system as a whole. When Olmsted arrived in Seattle in 1903, the first thing he did was go to the high points to get a view of the entire city and surrounding region. In that way he could ensure that the elements of the system would work together and within the larger context. Likewise, in designing a park or boulevard, Olmsted considered the surrounding areas and how they interacted with the designed landscape.

In a way that is surprisingly current more than a century later, Olmstedian landscapes are also responsive to the local environment. Although John Olmsted would not have used today's language of sustainability and environmental preservation, his

A double turn in the Lake Washington Boulevard.

Photo by Asahel Curtis

The drives and walks in these views of the upper bridge along Lake Washington Boulevard in Colman Park provide good examples of how circulation could be planned to benefit both pedestrians and drivers. Separating the grades enabled park visitors who wanted a quieter experience to walk down the ravine by passing under the bridge, while drivers could enjoy the ever-changing views as they made their way down the hill without having to watch too carefully for pedestrians. The meandering route of the drive also reinforces the naturalistic character of the park by following the contours of the topography rather than cutting into it with straight lines and sharp turns.

designs work with the existing local environment to ensure their success and longevity. He utilized native vegetation in designs and encouraged the Board of Park Commissioners to protect stands of trees and other vegetation. He waxed poetic about native vegetation in a letter to Sophie in 1906, writing, "The climate is so damp that everything grows luxuriantly. Brake ferns are higher than my head. The sallal [*sic*] rattles like starched linen when one walks through it." Unfamiliarity with the local environment did lead the firm astray occasionally. Scanning the plant lists associated with the different Seattle plans, one can find numerous references to English holly, English ivy, and other plants now considered invasive. Because

they grow so well in the Pacific Northwest, the plants were used widely by landscape architects and designers for slope stabilization and quickly filling in large areas with vegetation before the harm caused by their introduction was fully understood.

As Olmsted and his associates developed the Seattle park and boulevard system, these principles guided their work. Each park had its own character, determined by its natural characteristics and the role it played in the system. Their emphasis on park systems was an important part of why Olmsted was brought to Seattle. In their work on the Columbian Exposition the elder Olmsted, with John assisting him, had further developed his ideas for planning comprehensive systems of parks, shaping the land to create spaces that seemed natural but had been highly designed to achieve a particular effect, and improving American cities through the application of landscape architecture principles.

The desire to improve cities through landscape design extended beyond physical beauty and opportunities for recreation. The senior Olmsted wrote extensively about how providing access to nature and respites from the city would counteract the degrading effects of urbanization and improve the moral character of people from all social and economic classes. In a democracy, the health of the republic relied on the moral health of the voting population, so providing spaces like parks that would build strong moral character and bring the community together was an essential part of creating a modern city.

Planning with a comprehensive view was a new idea in American cities. Up until then, cities more often grew in a haphazard fashion. Industry occupied level land near transportation infrastructure, retail businesses mixed with light industry, often occupying street-level spaces in factory buildings, and open-space planning was largely nonexistent. Residences were interspersed with commercial buildings, their distance from noise- and pollution-generating businesses varying depending on the occupants' financial status. In the absence of mass transit, most people lived within walking distance of their workplaces. As transportation modes changed or population growth overran available housing, the cities adapted on an ad hoc basis.

As the 19th century progressed, several trends came together, and the idea of guiding city development to improve living conditions and promote economic development gained currency. What would become the City Beautiful movement had its roots in the Columbian Exposition in Chicago in 1893. The director of that world's fair, architect Daniel Burnham, used the exposition to showcase how architecture, landscape design, and planned development could create the "White City"—a beautiful, orderly, functional space that contrasted sharply with many chaotic and disorderly urban areas at that time, not the least of which was Chicago itself.

The Panic of 1893, which played a role in sidelining Schwagerl's plan for Seattle's park system, put civic improvements and further development of the City Beautiful movement on hold across the country. It would be nearly a decade before it would gain momentum and have enough influence with civic leaders to result in projects and initiatives. After the turn of the century, City Beautiful found a ready audience in Seattle. With its influence, the park system concept that had been bandied about for a decade snapped into focus as a tool for propelling the city forward in its development and its standing among American cities.

By 1903, in spite of a challenging history when it came to park development, Seattle was an ideal city to put Olmstedian design principles to work. Rarely did any of the Olmsteds get to work in a place just as it was developing. In Louisville, Boston, and other cities, they had to carve space for parks and parkways out of established neighborhoods and sprawling business and industrial districts. In Seattle,

Photographs taken by John Olmsted in May 1903 of the Lake Union shoreline (top) and the area south of the University of Washington campus where the Montlake neighborhood is today (bottom).

ADMINISTRATION BUILDING MAY 1. 1893

Administration Building in the Court of Honor at the World's Columbian Exposition in Chicago, 1893.

John Olmsted had a relatively open landscape, a cadre of park commissioners and other civic leaders eager to work with him, and the underlying currents of the public park and City Beautiful movements to prime the public for his plans. Olmsted drew on this foundation and used his time in Seattle in 1903 to develop a system that would serve the needs of existing neighborhoods and shape future residential development, identify Seattle's unique landscape features, and accommodate the city's infrastructure and industries.

Souvenir Map of the World's Columbian Exposition showing the layout of the "White City" that inspired the City Beautiful movement.

Study for parks and parkways by John Olmsted and Percy Jones in April and May 1903, using a 1901 base map. Colors show proposed parks in blue, proposed boulevards in green, existing parkland in orange, and other public property in yellow. This working plan is the best illustration of the 1903 Olmsted Park and Parkway System proposal.

CHAPTER 3
OLMSTED COMES TO SEATTLE

One of Olmsted's first reports home to Sophie after he arrived in Seattle on April 30, 1903, was, "I saw Mt. Rainier for the first time. It is huge." His letters, field notes, and quotes to the newspapers over the next five weeks would be filled with appraisals of the plants, trees, views, waterways, and other aspects of Seattle's landscape. The park system plan he would develop featured a diverse, interconnected mix of parks and parkways, each designed to capture different aspects of the remarkable natural beauty within the city and visible in the distance.

On his first morning in the city, Olmsted began with a trip to the top of the county courthouse, then located on what was known as Court House Hill, where Harborview Medical Center is today. He and his entourage of his assistant Percy Jones, Captain Pratt, and several of the park commissioners then crossed the city and climbed to the top of the

Washington Hotel on Denny Hill. These elevated views allowed Olmsted to see the lay of the land and the various existing and proposed waterways.

The group traversed large swaths of the city. From Denny Hill, they continued on to Capitol Hill to see Lincoln Park (Cal Anderson Park today) and Volunteer Park, and then to Madison Park, at that time a private park on Lake Washington. There they boarded a small motorboat and visited what they called the "Golf Club" on the northeast side of Union Bay on the lake. Jones also kept field notes recording their impressions and detailed information, such as street layout specifications provided by Captain Pratt.

Each day of the ensuing week, Olmsted and Jones followed a similar pattern: meet up with commissioners or other city officials in the morning, inspect a different sector of the city, including areas outside the city limits, and attend meetings, dinners,

Party touring Seattle with Olmsted at the shoreline of Lake Washington on May 1, 1903. From left to right: E. F. Blaine, Captain Pratt, E. F. Fuller, John C. Olmsted, Percy R. Jones, C. W. Saunders, J. E. Shrewsbury, A. L. Walters.

Two photographs, taken in May 1903, of the west side of Smith Cove from Galer Street on Queen Anne Hill (top, by John Olmsted) and of Bailey Peninsula (later Seward Park) across Andrews Bay (bottom).

and gatherings with civic leaders and government officials in the afternoon and evening. They traveled by streetcars and boats and, often, on foot. Olmsted and Jones took photographs and noted topographical characteristics of the ground they covered, soil conditions, existing trees and other vegetation, and existing infrastructure, especially noting components of the water system. The city's newspapers updated their readers regularly on which area of the city he had explored and with whom he had met.

They also assessed the work already completed or in progress at Kinnear, Denny, and Volunteer Parks. In Kinnear Park, Olmsted praised the trees in his field notes, but added in a letter to Sophie about Schwagerl's work in Denny and Kinnear Parks that "his walks are very crooked often & his banks steep & high and his planting very mixed but pretty much the same selection for every place." He went on to further criticize Schwagerl, writing to Sophie, "I saw some private places (on 1st Hill next east of the business center) on Sunday afternoon which he had graded and planted. In those he used large boulder banks for picturesque effect no matter whether the house was Old Colonial or American or Italian. So he seems to be no very considerable artist in his line." In contrast, he proclaimed the privately owned Ravenna Park a "very beautiful natural park" and recommended very few improvements for it.

Olmsted walked along the bicycle path system and took stock of the routes and their surroundings. Those paths took them around the undeveloped slopes of Capitol Hill's northern end and to one of the park locations Schwagerl recommended in 1892—

Electric railway car and station of the Seattle, Renton & Southern Railway Co. at Rainier Beach, ca. 1905.

BEFORE LEAVING SEATTLE, DON'T FAIL TO SEE

Ravenna or Big Tree Park

IT IS WORLD-FAMOUS. ❧ ASK ABOUT IT

TO REACH THE PARK—Take "Eastlake" car on Third Avenue marked "Ravenna Park," or take auto. It is only seven blocks north from Exposition Grounds

Ravenna Park brochure encouraging Alaska-Yukon-Pacific Exposition visitors to see the park while in Seattle.

Fort Lawton in Magnolia. He didn't visit the Alki Point or Sand Point park locations, likely because Alki Point was then in the city of West Seattle and Sand Point was quite far removed from the developed parts of Seattle. To visit Bailey Peninsula, then outside the city limits, but perhaps seeming more a part of the city because of its proximity to the Seattle, Renton & Southern Railway, which ran south from downtown Seattle through the Rainier Valley, Olmsted took the streetcar and then walked a considerable distance along the lakeshore.

In their walks and conversations with park commissioners and with each other, Olmsted and Jones evaluated the landscape in terms of how people would experience it. They looked for viewpoints, groves of trees, and grades that could be easily traversed on foot or in a carriage (cars had not yet arrived in Seattle in any significant number). While not averse to regrading the terrain, planting ornamentals and specimen plants and trees, or rerouting water features, Olmsted first looked for existing features that could be incorporated into the system or into park or parkway designs. Jones remarked in his field notes that the view at 35th Avenue and Cherry Street was "the finest I have seen of Lake Washington, and it would be a great objective point for people who wished a clear and unobstructed view of the Cascade Mountains and Mt Rainier." At Ravenna Park, Olmsted wrote, "the banks of the brook to Green Lake should be secured to keep the brook from contamination as well as to make a connection." On Beacon Hill, Jones remarked that a lot near 14th Avenue afforded a "very commanding view of the Olympic Range," while the view from the nearby city-owned land was obscured by the West Seattle peninsula intruding into the sightline.

Olmsted and Jones looked for land that would be less expensive to acquire and would help shape future development in the "suburbs" of the city—those neighborhoods outside the already-developed city center, built at the ends of streetcar lines that stretched like long fingers out from downtown. They found at Lake Dell (near Leschi) that the area was "pretty well filled up with cheap houses and their yards and pastures but might not be too costly to include." Acquiring such properties would limit their impact on nearby residences, parks, and parkways. While this may seem contrary to the democratic character of the City Beautiful movement and Olmstedian principles, it was a function of balancing the need for playgrounds and parks in the most distressed parts of the city, such as Pioneer Square, with the high cost of land in those densely populated neighborhoods and the desire to separate parkland from industrial areas.

Olmsted also wanted to ensure that the park system incorporated landscape features (such as views) along the shorelines and hilltops, away from the central city.

In walking on the hills, he noted the topography and the challenges it could pose for residential development. In his December 1903 report to the Portland park board on their park system, Olmsted described how residential developments on steep hillsides would inevitably be inferior because the land was undesirable and so, at first, only cheap housing with minimal infrastructure would be built. Then, he warned, as land grew scarcer in the city, the hills would become more attractive and the city would have to make significant investments to bring it up to standard with retaining walls, streets with reasonable grades, and sidewalks. To prevent this situation, Olmsted recommended to the Portland park commissioners that the city

take these lands out of the market for residential purposes, and use them for pleasure grounds for the benefit of the citizens at large, and for the particular benefit of adjoining properties above and below. In that case all those who would have built houses on the uneconomical sites will build them elsewhere, and with easier conditions will build handsomer and better houses, or more of them, greatly to the benefit of the taxable valuation of the city.

From his remarks and notes in Seattle, it appears he held the same views regarding its hills.

On May 11, 1903, Olmsted spoke before the Seattle city council. According to *The Seattle Times*, he urged them to acquire more land for parks and parkways because "the lands so far secured do not

Photograph of view downhill to Leschi Park and across Lake Washington taken by Percy Jones in May 1903.

contain the best tracts and the choicest places, full of the natural beauties that will all too soon be turned into building lots unless taken by the city." He used Boston as a cautionary tale, explaining how that city had incurred enormous expense in replanting trees and vegetation on shorelines in its parks because so much had been cleared away before the land could be acquired. The paper quoted Olmsted as saying:

Your harbor front must be devoted to commerce, but around Lake Washington, Green Lake and other fresh water bodies there is an abundance of park possibilities, such views of wooded hills and outside views that are seldom met with. These lands, too, are going so fast that the city right now should take advantage of the time to secure them before they are all occupied or the native woods cut away.

After Jones had been in Seattle for a couple of weeks, it appears that he saw the Schwagerl plan, although he attributes it to Pratt in his field notes. Jones' comments focused on the shoreline survey work shown on the plan, primarily on the route the lakeshore boulevard would take if the lake was to be lowered, and he questioned whether an alignment along the exposed new land or back from

TALKS ABOUT SEATTLE PARKS

Expert From Boston Sees Unusual Advantages Here

ADDRESS TO ENGINEERS

John C. Olmsted Discusses Fine Chance to Beautify City, Especially Near the Water

SHOULD PRESERVE THE TREES

John C. Olmsted, the landscape gardener from Boston, who is in Seattle for the purpose of forming a systematic plan for parks, spoke before the Pacific Northwest Society of Engineers at the Chamber of Commerce last night, upon the importance of parks, play grounds, beautiful drives and recreation grounds to a city.

"You have most unusual advantages in Seattle in this regard," said Mr. Olmsted. "Nature has been most lavish, and if you are wise, you will begin now to preserve some of the natural beauty of the scenery. Along the shores of Elliott bay and Lake Union and Washington you have an opportunity to lay out some of the most beautiful drives in the country.

"Don't make the mistake made by the early settlers of nearly every one of our large cities, by cutting down all the trees as a nuisance, and making the ground bare. Our forefathers did just that in Boston, and destroyed practically all of the scenic beauty of the islands around that city. The people who live in Boston today, know that a mistake was made then, and even now they are talking of planting trees on the islands and doing something to beautify the ground along the water front.

"By all means the fringes along your lakes and the bay, if possible, should be set aside for public use. Commerce has a large claim upon the water front, as a matter of course, but you have such an immense lot of land fronting upon lake and bay that there is ample room for commerce and pleasure grounds. Along your lake fronts, for example, the city can acquire land now for a small cost, that will be almost invaluable in years to come.

"Your opportunities for boating in this city are unsurpassed. You will find as the city grows older, and the inhabitants grow more settled, and wealth is acquired, that the people will flock to the water during the summer months. Boston has more private pleasure craft than any city in this country, yet the opportunities for boating around Boston are not to be compared to those of this city.

"In years to come you will find your men of wealth building homes in the suburbs. In this respect Seattle is unsurpassed in facilities. You can get now for a trifling cost, what other cities in the country would be willing to pay almost any price to acquire.

"I think the street car companies, the telegraph and telephone companies, who make such large use of the streets, should be taxed and the money expended for parking systems. That is done in Baltimore, so that the parks do not cost the public 1 cent. We have altogether too few play grounds in our cities. Boston common was originally intended for a cow pasture, so that the fathers do not deserve any especial credit for its preservation.

"As it is a well-known fact that property abutting on a park or boulevard, wider than the ordinary street, is more valuable than when facing on the regulation street, it is perhaps but fair that part of the expense should be borne by abutting property."

Besides the members of the society there were a large number of heavy taxpayers who listened to the remarks of Mr. Olmsted. Judge McGilvra was invited to speak, and he called attention to the fact that about ten years ago the city paid an architect $10,000 to lay out a system of parks, boulevards, play grounds and lovers' rambles. The plans were very elaborate, and he had opposed them for more than a year. He had not heard of them for several years past, and he thought City Engineer Thomson, who is also president of the society, should drag them from their hiding place, and ask Mr. Olmsted what be thinks of them.

President Thomson promised to do so, and apropos of valuable public records becoming mislaid, he introduced A. Y. Bouillon, who read a very able paper upon the subject of "Indexing and Filing Office Drawing Records."

This May 1903 Seattle Post-Intelligencer *article reports on Olmsted's talk to the Pacific Northwest Society of Engineers, one of the many talks he gave to community groups to build public support for the park system he was developing.*

The newly built Hotel Washington Annex, where Percy Jones stayed while in Seattle.

the shoreline 50 or 75 feet above water level would be preferable, given that he did not think any trees should be cut from the existing shoreline. Jones made no mention of showing the plan to Olmsted, and Schwagerl's system plan is not referenced elsewhere in the field notes or in correspondence.

In addition to working out the park system plan, Olmsted made several public appearances to explain his work. He spoke on May 2 to the Pacific Northwest Society of Engineers, and on May 25 he shared his ideas with the Chamber of Commerce. *The Seattle Times* reported that the Chamber leadership then asked the city's improvement clubs to help build support for the park system among their members.

The improvement clubs were a key component of garnering public support, and they would play a significant role in the implementation of the park and boulevard system over the next decade. In an era when city government's role was fairly limited in terms of land use and economic development, the neighborhood-based improvement clubs emerged as miniature chambers of commerce. Property and business owners and boosters for their neighborhoods, club members worked to get the city to invest in infrastructure and to attract new businesses and residents. Each club had a vision for how their neighborhood should develop, depending on its particular advantages, such as a waterway for

1904 University of Washington Plan

Before the city approached the Olmsted Brothers to work on a city park system, the University of Washington's Board of Regents contacted the firm in 1902 about working on a campus plan. They corresponded, but the regents did not formally hire the firm until Olmsted's visit in the spring of 1903. He submitted his preliminary plan in late December 1904. It featured an arts quadrangle and a science quadrangle and a number of playfields and a large athletic field where Husky Stadium is today. The parkway from Washington Park entered the campus about where the eastern end of the Montlake Cut is today, then turned northwest to climb the hill, reaching approximately the alignment of today's Stevens Way along the eastern side of campus then continuing along a curving route all the way to the northern border of the campus, near today's 21st Avenue NE. Olmsted felt strongly that the parkway should extend through the campus, thereby incorporating it into the city's park system.

The campus plan reserved ample open space for the public to enjoy, particularly along the Lake Washington and Lake Union shorelines. Olmsted wrote to Alden J. Blethen, president of the Board of Regents, "We believe it will be of distinct advantage to the University and an unquestionable benefit to the city at large to carry a parkway through the eastern part of the University grounds on the bluffs overlooking Lake Washington . . . the parkway will provide the most delightful and dignified way of driving to and from the University and the city." He also believed the university would benefit from the exposure to parkway users who would also be important supporters of the future development of the school.

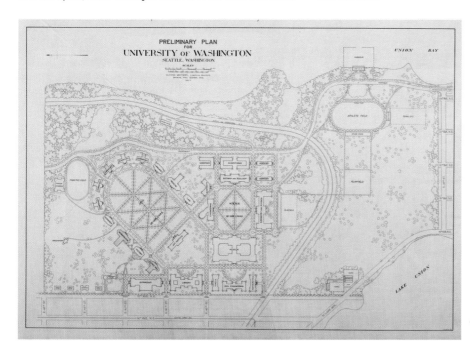

Preliminary Plan for University of Washington campus, 1904.

55

Mount Baker Improvement Club members on New Year's Day, 1912.

industrial development, a private park, or a ferry landing. The clubs worked with other improvement clubs to promote the city as a whole or to boost citywide improvements and often coordinated donations of land for parks and playgrounds.

On May 18, not quite three weeks after arriving in Seattle, Olmsted recorded in his field notes that he had the plan sketched out. He and Jones made calculations of the acreage required and then estimated the cost of acquiring each parcel. By the end of the month they had identified an initial list of priority acquisitions for a total cost of $1,193,000, significantly more than the $500,000 in bonds the park board could ask voters to approve for initial park work.

Olmsted and Jones met with the park commissioners and the Superintendent of Streets and Parks Abraham L. Walters on May 29 and worked out a reduced system that the city could fund in the near future.

After a few more excursions around the city, Olmsted departed for Cheyenne, Wyoming, on June 5. He took the Seattle report with him to finish making revisions and sent it to the Board of Park Commissioners on July 2. As with every plan he developed, he sent a report that provided a narrative description of its elements and summarized the thinking behind it. A newspaper article mentions that the report was accompanied by maps showing the alignments of the boulevards and the locations of parks, but no records of those maps are found in the Olmsted Brothers' records held at the Frederick Law Olmsted National Historic Site.

Calculations of proposed park system acquisition costs made by Percy Jones on May 29, 1903.

Photograph of shoreline below Madrona Park showing streetcar line, likely taken by Percy Jones in May 1903.

The 86-page report explained in detail what the park and boulevard system should encompass and offered the "reduced system" alternative for the commission so they could get started on the parts they could reasonably expect to fund in the near term. Olmsted began his report with praise for the local landscape:

> *Seattle possesses extraordinary landscape advantages in having a great abundance and variety of water views and views of wooded hills and distant mountains and snow-capped peaks. It also possesses within its boundaries, or close to them, some valuable remains of the original evergreen forests which covered the whole country, and which, aside from the grand size of some of the trees composing them, have very dense and beautiful undergrowth.*

The system he designed was intended to "secure and preserve for the use of the people as much as possible of these advantages of water and mountain views and of woodlands, well distributed and conveniently located." He noted that rising land values on property adjacent to developed parks and parkways would raise tax revenue that could be used to acquire more land and improve it, particularly

Montlake Ditch log canal through the Montlake isthmus from the east side, ca. 1900.

if those who owned the land were "helpful and co-operative" and did not insist upon "every cent possible for the needed land."

In the first section of the report, Olmsted described the park system elements in the order they would be experienced by someone traveling along the boulevards, starting at Bailey Peninsula in the southeast corner. That tract, he wrote, should be acquired for its land, "uniformly and beautifully covered with woods."

Moving north, he called for a strip of land large enough for drives and walks with a "foreground of woods" extending from the peninsula to the city boundary at Hanford Street. From there to Madrona Park, he included the entire hillside and shoreline in the plan, with enough room at the top of the hill for a "crestline parkway." From Madrona Park to the north side of the Denny-Blaine Addition, today's Thomas Street, he recommended that a strip of shoreland between 100 and 200 feet wide be reserved, and

then the parkland would widen back out again to encompass the hillside from there to the Firloch Club, where the Seattle Tennis Club is located today.

The parkway continued northwest from this section, crossing over to Washington Park via a saddle in the hill and running through the park and what was known as the Montlake Portage to the University of Washington campus. Following the crest of the hill on the east side of the campus, the boulevard would meander northward to Ravenna Park and then climb the hill to the brook draining Green Lake.

Following the brook, the parkway would join up with the existing parkway around the east and north sides of Green Lake to a new section on its western shore, then pass through Woodland Park and follow the slope down from the park's northwest corner into Ross, between Fremont and Ballard. At 14th Avenue, it would cross over the planned ship canal, travel through Interbay, then traverse the opposite slope to a point overlooking Smith Cove from the west, "which commands a very fine view of the city, harbor sound and mountains." Curving around Magnolia, Olmsted wanted the entire bluff and beach extending to Fort Lawton brought into the system. He believed, "It can safely be assumed that Fort Lawton Reservation will have various pleasure drives laid out in it, and that its use by the public as a pleasure ground will always be permitted by the United States authorities." This series of parks from Bailey Peninsula to Fort Lawton, connected by the boulevard, formed a string of parks and "attenuated parks" that, including loop drives on the peninsula and in the military base, measured 23¾ miles.

Bicycle path in Magnolia, near Fort Lawton (today's Discovery Park).

To this basic framework, Olmsted added several branch parkways. One departed from the lakeshore boulevard at Mount Baker, climbing up into the Rainier Valley and then continuing on to the northeast corner of Beacon Hill Park to connect with the Pipe Line road (so-named for the city's water system supply pipe running under it) that bisected the park, which itself would be made into a boulevard with divided lanes for ordinary traffic, pleasure driving, and a speedway. From the southern end of the pipeline road, a parkway would drop down into the Duwamish River valley via a southwesterly route and end at the "new driving park," which was likely the Meadows race track. He recommended expanding the park to include a nearby meadow for field games.

Several other parkways climbed Seattle's hills from the main pleasure drive. One would leave the drive in Washington Park and pass through the "beautifully wooded ravines" to Volunteer Park, if the property owners would provide "cordial assistance" to the park commissioners in acquiring the necessary right-of-way. Two others would branch off the main parkway, which continued around to the south side of Magnolia just after crossing the canal right-of-way. One would travel around the north side of Queen Anne Hill and "bend into the ravines and out around the spurs until it reaches the top of the steep bluff at the corner of Howe street and Taylor avenue," then continue around and up to the water tower at the top of the hill. The other Queen Anne parkway would extend from Interbay, sloping up the west side of Queen Anne Hill to Kinnear Park. As he had recommended for parts of the Lake Washington parkway, the slopes below the parkway on both sides of the hill were to be included in the park system.

Olmsted had identified some additional tracts of land that could be incorporated into the system. One was a branch parkway along the slope forming the eastern side of the Rainier Valley, running from an undetermined point south of Hanford Street to join up with the crest parkway along the lake. His concern about "an undesirable class of occupation" appears again in his advice to acquire the low ground at the north end of Union Bay to prevent its development with low-quality housing.

Photograph of the north side of Queen Anne Hill taken by Percy Jones in May 1903.

He then described a series of properties that he urged the city to acquire before it was too late, whether because the trees would be cleared, the views blocked, or the real estate too expensive. They were located throughout the city, from the peninsula jutting into the north end of Lake Union (today's Gas Works Park) to viewpoints at East Cherry and 25th Avenue, McGraw and 7th Avenue West, and the old reservoir on Beacon Hill. For playgrounds, Olmsted identified lots at 4th Avenue and Mercer Street, Jefferson Street and 13th Avenue, and Rainier Avenue and Charles Street. Despite considerable searching along the harbor, he found only a couple of suitable places for a saltwater park in downtown: one at the foot of Battery Street and another at the foot of Denny Way.

Olmsted ended the description of Seattle's comprehensive system with an explanation for the absence of large parks:

Considering the extent of the land which should be secured in connection with the informal portions of the parkway above described, and considering the size and beauty of the several large natural bodies of water thus made available, and considering the existing parks and the semi-public pleasure ground of the State University and Fort Lawton, it seems unnecessary to

Borrowed Landscapes

Olmsted wrote in his 1908 supplemental report for Seattle, "There is some question whether, considering the tremendous natural advantages of the Sound and the lakes, it will be necessary that the city should have anywhere within its present boundaries a park of this class." He was referring to parks of the sixth class, or those in which a "considerable body of natural landscape is preserved." Instead, Olmsted would repeatedly locate parks and parkways to take advantage of "borrowed landscapes." By framing views of distant features, such as the Olympic Mountains or Puget Sound, Olmsted could bring them into the landscape design and provide a more expansive sense of space. This contrasts with park designs Olmsted did for other cities in which curving paths and view corridors within parks make use of obscured end points to make a space seem larger than it actually is.

The view to the northwest from Jefferson Park includes the city skyline, Elliott Bay, and the Queen Anne Hill and Magnolia neighborhoods.

provide, for the period of a generation at least, one or more large parks.

This contrasted with park system plans for other cities, such as Brooklyn or Buffalo, which included at least one large (more than 500 acres) park.

Olmsted then turned his attention to the likelihood that the Board of Park Commissioners would issue bonds for $500,000 (with the approval of voters). For that amount, and with donations and below-market prices from at least some of the sellers, he believed they could develop a reduced system for the short term. Instead of beginning the parkway at Bailey Peninsula, he started it at Beacon Hill Park (Jefferson Park today). This section would run down the hill, across the valley, and then down to the lakeshore where Mount Baker Park is today and continue north from there. After passing through Washington Park, a "Union Bay Parkway" would continue over to the university campus. An extension and widening of Pine Grove Boulevard, the street then forming the southern boundary of Woodland Park, would connect Woodland Park with the university campus instead of traveling between Ravenna Park and Green Lake along the brook. He kept the Volunteer Hill Parkway spur, connecting Volunteer and Washington Parks, with a right-of-way wide enough to "include the best portions of the wooded ravines, and enough of the bluffs west of Tenth avenue to control the view." Two more parkways, Kinnear and Magnolia Bluffs, would connect Kinnear Park with Magnolia across Interbay and Fort Lawton. Magnolia would also be reached from Ballard via the Thorndyke Boulevard parkway.

In the next section, Olmsted called for the construction of three playgrounds, with funds coming from the city's general fund rather than the park fund, if needed. He prioritized the Mercer Street, Jefferson Street, and Rainier Avenue playgrounds because "they are close to or surrounded by a large population of a class most requiring such playgrounds, and because these sites are now vacant, but are likely to be occupied by dwellings within a few years if not soon secured." One of the reasons the public supported park development was the belief that access to parks improved the moral character of poor people. As an editorial in *The Seattle Republican* explained,

Children must have recreation; force them to find it in the public streets and the moral standing of the future citizen is lowered. A little closer attention to the making of good citizens out of the rising generations, to safeguard them from becoming physical and moral wrecks, a benefit, instead of a hindrance in the advancement of the community is a part of the duty man owes to his fellow man.

In particular, those children whose families could not afford to go to the mountains or Hood Canal or another resort-type spot needed access to parks. Support of playgrounds would grow significantly in the 1900s, and Olmsted would include more of them in his later Seattle plans.

Olmsted was strategic in his planning to ensure that the Board of Park Commissioners could provide the greatest possible benefit to the city for the intended $500,000 bond issue. He explained that the focus on parkway development in the reduced plan was because, if the comprehensive system could be developed in the near future, then

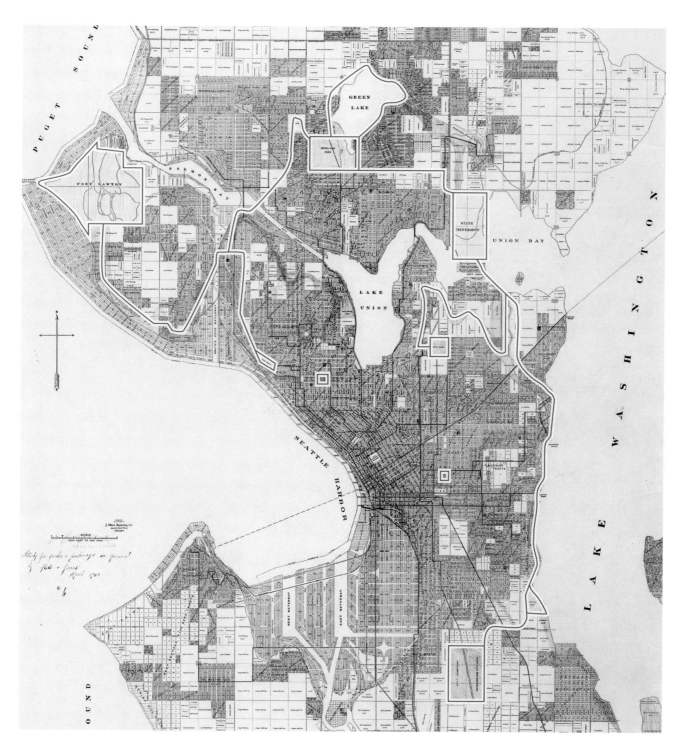

The reduced system recommended by Olmsted, shown above, identified those portions of the full plan that could be purchased with $500,000 in park bonds, which was the amount that the Board of Park Commissioners could put before the voters in the near term. Completing the reduced system would build support for additional park bonds, which could be used to fund the full plan.

the proposed parkways are located so as to be of the greatest possible immediate advantage to the existing population, as well as to secure for all time convenient access to a great number of exceedingly fine view points, to preserve sufficient areas of the beautiful natural woods, and to provide a sufficiently continuous and long series of pleasure drives, bridle paths and bicycle paths, which purpose cannot be accomplished at all satisfactorily in the existing parks, nor even by a much less extensive parkway system than that suggested.

The next section of the report provided fairly detailed descriptions of the proposed parks and

This Board of Park Commissioners brochure on Seattle parks and playgrounds illustrates the extent to which playgrounds would develop over the next few years.

parkways of the comprehensive plan. It explained the route of the primary parkway and the parks associated with it as it would loop its way around the city. For the parkways, he described the routes they should follow, and how they should enter, traverse, and exit the large existing parks. Most of the discussion of the routes addressed the views, the need to follow the shoreline, and the land that would have to be acquired to protect the views. For some sections, he offered several alternative routes. He warned that "a pleasure drive laid out on a succession of straight lines would be exceedingly ugly, awkward and undesirable" and pointed to Maynard's Lake Washington subdivision as an example of the unfortunate results of private landowners laying out the lakeshore drive. He emphasized the need to make streets curvilinear to match the topography of their surroundings and reminded the City that it made no sense to apply the standard rectangular street grid to steep lands.

Olmsted repeatedly warned against allowing the steep areas along the lake and elsewhere in the city to be developed for residences. There had already been some serious landslides along the lake. One in 1901 carried the Taylor Mill and a number of houses into the lake. Olmsted made a case for incorporating the entire slide area from about South Holgate Street to South Lane Street, known as the Rainier Heights area, writing that "there will be no end to the trouble, expense and inconvenience due to the continuation of the slide if it is allowed to become occupied by houses." He described the inevitability of broken sewer lines and water pipes when future slides occurred and the city's liability. In contrast, if the area

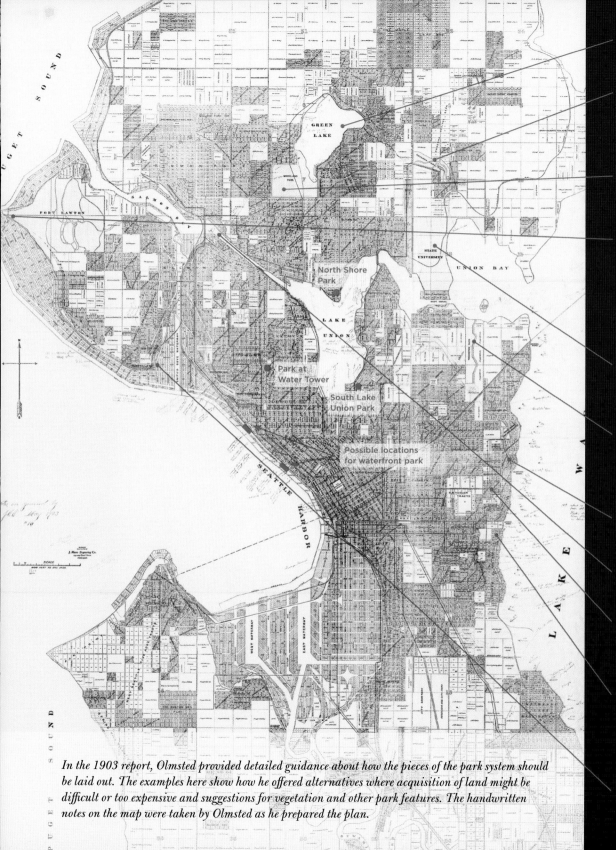

In the 1903 report, Olmsted provided detailed guidance about how the pieces of the park system should be laid out. The examples here show how he offered alternatives where acquisition of land might be difficult or too expensive and suggestions for vegetation and other park features. The handwritten notes on the map were taken by Olmsted as he prepared the plan.

"At three or four places on the east side of the lake, where the curves of the boulevard are convex toward the lake, points of land should be filled out...sufficient to afford space for considerable groups of trees."

"A liberal strip of land of varying width should be taken to include the brook which flows from Green Lake and through Ravenna Park, and particularly the banks of the ravine which extends up the brook several blocks west of the park...it would not involve very heavy grading to divert the brook so as to make Latona and Tahoe avenues form the border streets."

"The main parkway should be continued through Woodland Park by means of a drive, bridle path, bicycle path and walk so located on curves adapted to the local topography as to form part of a proper system for the development of the park."

"This beach is broad and sandy and probably the only one, and certainly the best one for bathing within an equal distance of the city. The privilege for using it for this purpose should be secured from the government." At the park, Olmsted recommended running the parkway along the eastern border, but on "agreeable curvilinear lines." The parkway would then turn west at the north end of the park and follow the shoreline, which he recommended the city purchase to protect views, to the university campus on the north side of the proposed ship canal."

"An imaginary boundary...should be arranged for so that subsequent officials of the University cannot thoughtlessly or otherwise interfere with the slopes and plantations along the west side of the drive, or insist upon allowing the trees to grow up thickly east of the drive, thus blocking the view."

"The east boundary [of Washington Park] should be on agreeable curvilinear lines, so adapted to the topography as to provide for a border street on good grades and curves...The park should also be extended further east along the shore of Union Bay, Foster Island and all rights to the land under water in front of the park should be secured."

"In order to provide an agreeable park connection between the lake and Washington Park, a width of five hundred and six hundred feet should be secured west of Thirty-eighth avenue."

"It would desirable, if not too expensive, to carry the parkway over the Fremont-Ballard street railway by a bridge and to continue it on a high level across the lowland between it and the government canal."

The boulevard from Yesler Way to Madrona Park, "besides giving to the fullest extent the pleasant effect of driving through the midst of dense woods, would afford occasional picturesque glimpses of the distant landscape through the trees below, which could be sufficiently trimmed or thinned for this purpose."

"Considering the experience of other cities with similar parkways along the crests of hills commanding similar views, there can be no doubt that, whatever the cost of this parkway may be, it will be far more than repaid to the city." But if that acquisition proved impossible, then "preserv[ing] the fringe of trees growing along the shore...would form practically an enlargement of Leschi Park southward."

"The plan and location of the main parkway from Thirteenth avenue and Nickerson avenue to a point west of Smith's Cove...will be on formal lines, fitted closely to the existing subdivisions."

was a park, slides could be easily accommodated with simple repairs to drives and paths.

Olmsted was much less specific regarding the locations or development of the small parks discussed in this section of the report. Depending on different factors, the park commissioners could choose one or more locations for small parks on the south and east sides of Lake Union. For the rest of the city, he wrote, "If the needed land for local parks at various places where there are fine views, and where there are opportunities for playgrounds, are not secured in connection with the system of parkways, they should be secured as independent small parks. Except to thus call attention to them, it will be unnecessary to describe them individually as they have already been sufficiently referred to in describing the general parkway system."

For playgrounds, however, he recommended six specific locations: Mercer Street at 3rd Avenue, Jefferson Street east of Broadway, Rainier Avenue and 16th Avenue, a two-block tract in North Queen Anne, East Cherry Street at 25th Avenue (Garfield Playfield), and Fremont Shore, the point jutting into Lake Union between the two arms of the lake (today's Gas Works Park). He gave varying directives, from just a recommendation to acquire land as soon as possible on Queen Anne to detailed plans he provided for developing the Rainier Valley playground.

The final section of the report addressed the existing city parks. Olmsted gave recommendations regarding the size, layout, vegetation, and character of the parks. A recurring theme in his discussion of the city parks is variation. Each park, Olmsted emphasized, should respond to its particular setting, conditions, and surroundings—its "genius of place." He wrote, "The different parts of the city should not be made to look as much like each other as possible, but on the contrary every advantage should be taken of differing conditions to give each one a distinct individuality of its own." Denny Park should be distinct in its plantings from Kinnear Park, and Volunteer Park should be unique as well, with differences in the varieties of plants, their arrangement, and the amenities offered.

For Capitol Hill's Lincoln Park, he addressed the section south of the reservoir. He wanted the city to expand the park to connect it more directly with Broadway High School, located one-half block to the west. If they could acquire the row of lots between the park and Broadway, then the high school could anchor the east-west axis of the park's design and the north-south axis could align with the reservoir's gatehouse. Neighbors had complained about the open area south of the reservoir being used as an ad hoc baseball field, and so Olmsted recommended a fairly formal design with hedges and lawns and space for "lawn tennis and other quiet lawn games."

In Woodland Park, Olmsted was primarily concerned about the streetcar line. Cutting across the hillside on an elevated trestle, it disrupted the park experience with its noise. To mitigate the impact, he called for building up banks under the tracks and adding stone walls extending up from the top of the banks to the level of the streetcars' windows. This would dampen the noise of the wheels on the tracks, but still allow the streetcar riders to experience the park as they passed through it.

Seattle Electric Railway streetcar in Woodland Park, ca. 1910.

In Washington Park he gave instructions for managing the vegetation. Along the lakeshore, he thought the trees should be intermittently cleared to allow views out to the lake. On the steeper parts of the interior of the park, he thought all of the trees should be left standing, but in the lower parts he called for more clearing so that open, turfed areas could be developed to accommodate gatherings of people. He was concerned, too, about the brook running through the park, recommending a plan to supply it with city water if development dried up its natural sources and to keep it shaded so it would not become fetid in the summer.

The large park, as yet undeveloped, on Beacon Hill, known variously as Beacon Hill Park and City Park, offered an opportunity for preserving "wild growths" and for developing a baseball field. Knowing that baseball games would be the primary draw of the park, Olmsted recommended planting summer-blooming varieties that would be at their peak during baseball season. As he would in his later playfield designs, he included an area away from the field for groves of trees and strolling paths. The vegetation, he recommended, should be planted in layers so as to look like "irregular mounds of foliage," and the paths should be routed around the "mounds," with views to Lake Washington left open to provide glimpses out to the water (later development would block these views).

Somewhat surprisingly, he ended his report with three very small spaces. One, Somerville Park (Dearborn Park), was just five acres in the suburban development south of Beacon Hill Park called Somerville. It was covered with uncut forest, something that was already becoming scarce, and abutted 23 acres of similar forest that could be acquired. Likewise, he mentioned Beacon Park, a mere half-acre of land on the north end of Beacon Hill that he thought could be turfed and planted with shade trees until a later date when a more formal design with a fountain or statue could be implemented. The only downtown park mentioned was Pioneer Square, which Olmsted thought should be reserved for a monument to Seattle's early non-Native settlers.

In a letter sent to Blaine with the report on July 2, 1903, Olmsted wrote, "The work has interested us very much and we have derived a great deal of pleasure, not only from our intercourse with the commission and city officials, but from an examination of the extraordinarily beautiful landscape and the delightful woods." Olmsted and Jones' appreciation of the land and vegetation is apparent in the masterful interplay between the parks and parkways and the views, trees, water features, and topography in the plan. The spaces that Olmsted identified have proven remarkably enduring because of this close association with the "genius of place" of the different parts of the system and how they come together as a whole.

Pioneer Place, a small open space in the heart of downtown Seattle, was surrounded by streets filled with streetcar lines, wagons, and pedestrian traffic in 1903.

Volunteer Park Planting Plan (02695-43) developed by Olmsted in 1910, showing which flowers, shrubs, and trees should be located in the park's extensive planting beds.

CHAPTER 4
BUILDING A PARK SYSTEM

Just two months after bringing the Olmsted Brothers firm to Seattle, the Board of Park Commissioners had a comprehensive park system plan. To move forward on implementing it, the commissioners wanted the Seattle City Council to adopt the plan formally. That stamp of approval from the council, though not legally necessary, would provide a solid foundation for the commissioners to move forward with developing the existing parks, accepting donations of land for parks and parkways, and putting a bond measure to fund land purchases on the ballot. It would also make it clear to developers how their subdivisions should incorporate the plan. It would take several months for the council to adopt the plan, but once they did so, the park board would begin nearly a decade of rapid development of hundreds of acres of parks and miles of parkways that together would form the framework of a system

to serve the city of a half million people that Seattle hoped to become.

In anticipation of the report's release, the commissioners began drumming up public support for the system plan while Olmsted was still in Seattle in the spring of 1903. They had him speak to various groups in May and June about his vision for the park system, and the park commissioners visited improvement clubs' meetings to encourage their endorsements. The highly positive newspaper reports about these meetings did not indicate any opposition to the plan.

Despite this public support, the city council lagged in adopting the plan. In late September, more than two months after Olmsted sent the report to the park board, *The Seattle Times* reported, "The council has been very slow to act upon this report, which has been in the hands of the members for

Interlaken Boulevard, shown here in 1910, was one of the first elements of the park system developed.

many weeks." On October 3, 1903, the park and boulevard committee held a joint meeting with the finance committee to consider the plan, and they recommended full council approval. The next day, the *Seattle Post-Intelligencer* printed the full text of the Olmsted report on a large two-page spread with the bold headline "Olmsted's Elaborate System of Parkways Will Make Seattle a Most Beautiful City."

Newspaper coverage emphasized that the plan would only direct the Board of Park Commissioners' efforts to develop parkland, not mandate acquisitions or expenditures, and that property acquisitions would be made gradually. Articles in *The Seattle Times* also reassured readers that the park board would not be acquiring "valuable residence property and turning it into driveways and parks at great expense." Instead, the writer indicated, the least desirable land for residential development would be taken in almost all cases, and "Mr. Blaine, for the most part, looks upon it as the reclamation of shantytown land." In this era, neither zoning nor deed restrictions regulated property use. It was a significant concern for residential developers that one of their "suburbs," or neighborhoods outside the downtown core, could be blighted by existing or potential ad hoc developments of inexpensive housing that served the large population of working-class families in Seattle. Blaine wanted to reassure the wealthier property owners that the park system would encourage the development they wanted, while discouraging the kind they did not.

Despite these promises, some concerns arose over the impact the plan's implementation could have on already-platted subdivisions. When the plan came before the council for a vote on October 5, Oliver C. McGilvra, representing property owners of McGilvra's 1st and 2nd Additions, located near Lakeview Park today, opposed the plan's adoption until they could compare the proposal to a replat currently underway (at considerable expense) for neighborhood development along the boulevard between Lake Washington and Washington Park. Judge William H. Moore, former Superior Court judge, state senator, and property owner in the Lake Dell (Leschi) area, raised a similar concern. Contrary to what Olmsted had hoped, property owners would not always gladly donate land for park and parkway purposes. Some wanted to retain as much land as possible to profit from the higher prices they could command once parks or boulevards were developed adjacent to their parcels. The vote on adopting the plan was held over for two weeks to resolve these issues.

It would be more than a month before the plan finally came back to the full council for a vote on November 16, 1903. At that meeting, the council unanimously adopted the park system plan without any revisions. The council members and park commissioners interpreted the vote's import differently, however. Several council members remarked that the adoption would not have much practical influence. Park commissioner Blaine, on the other hand, believed that "the city will have something to work to, and it will not be many years before the effect will be seen." Within the week, developers eager with anticipation promoted house lots on Magnolia Bluff as being "along Olmsted's proposed Fort Lawton Boulevard."

OLMSTED'S ELABORATE SYSTEM OF PARKWAYS WILL MAKE SEATTLE A MOST BEAUTIFUL CITY

John C. Olmsted

A Comprehensive System of Parks and Parkways

Five Views of City

Reduced Section for the Slow Future

Dr. Baker Park

Description of Proposed Parks and Parkways

LAKE FRONT AT LESCHI PARK

IN MADRONA PARK

Rainier Heights Landslide Section

Washington Park to State University Grounds

University Grounds to Ravenna Park

Madrona Park to North End of Denny-Blaine Lake Park

Delta Way to Madrona Park

Woodland Park to Northwest Base of Queen Anne Hill

LAKE WASHINGTON FROM THE PORTAGE

Fort Lawton Reservation

Proposed Local Parks and Playgrounds

Volunteer Hill Parkway

LAKE WASHINGTON CYCLE PATH

Other Small Parks

Queen Anne Hill Parkway

Jefferson Street Playground

SCENE IN RAVENNA PARK

Woodland Park

Kinnear Park

The Seattle Post-Intelligencer *promoted adoption of Olmsted's park system plan by reprinting the text of his report in this two-page spread.*

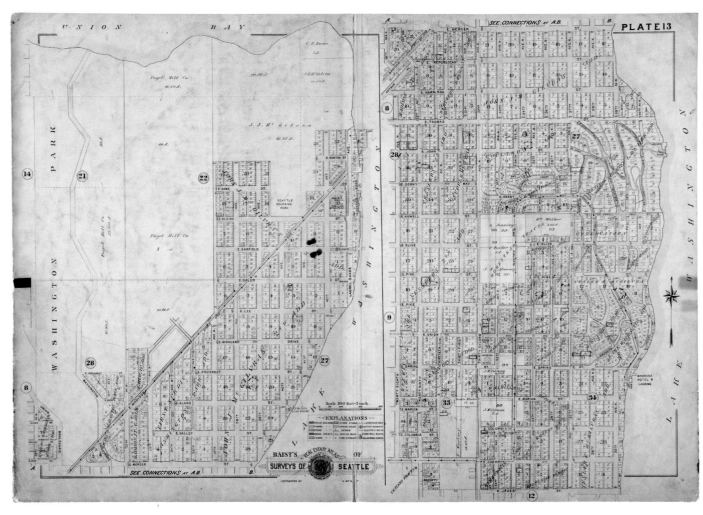

The proposed route of the plan's primary boulevard would pass through McGilvra's 1st and 2nd Additions, shown in the Baist map above, as it climbed the hill and traversed the ravine between Lake Washington and Washington Park.

With the park plan adopted, the park board's work turned to implementation. Commissioner Charles Saunders wrote to Olmsted on December 4, seeking his advice about hiring a park superintendent, developing plans for individual parks, and acquiring land. In reply, Olmsted wrote, "It seems to us that the most important step to be taken now in park matters is to secure a modification of the city charter by which the whole park business can be put in charge of a park commission working independently of the Common [City] Council as completely as is customary in most of the larger cities of this country." The park board needed real power to increase their budget and make decisions about acquisitions to carry out their work effectively. Olmsted recommended that the board be relatively small and led by a president who was a "man of marked business ability and wide experience . . . accustomed to managing large affairs and [capable] of getting the most of the work in connection with them done by competent employees." The other commissioners, he wrote, should be professional "men of good judgment and taste and broad experience and knowledge of park matters in many cities of this country and Europe." He recommended that the park board fund acquisition with long-term bonds, and that the maintenance budget be funded by a property tax.

The park board took Olmsted's suggestions and developed a proposed charter amendment that gave the board jurisdiction over the park fund, park management, and parks employees, including the superintendent. This last provision would remove the Superintendent of Streets, and thus the Board of Public Works, from any direct supervision of the Park Department. The council refused to put the amendment to the voters, believing it would give too much power to the park board. In response, the commissioners compromised and ceded the final approval of parkland acquisitions to the city council along with the power to set the annual levy rate between 75 cents and $1 per $1,000 in assessed value.

Even with these changes, the city council refused to put the charter amendment on the ballot, so the park board made use of a newly enacted state law allowing citizens to petition for a ballot measure to amend a city charter. They had to scramble to get enough signatures before the deadline, but they succeeded, and it was placed on the ballot for the

March 8, 1904, election. *The Seattle Times* and *Seattle Post-Intelligencer* actively supported the amendment on their editorial pages and noted that concerns over financial dealings were unfounded since the board would not actually handle the cash in the park fund. *The Seattle Star* reported on the details of the proposed amendment and the controversy that ensued when City Engineer R. H. Thomson, who actively opposed the amendment, sent a letter to the newspapers warning that a yes vote meant giving financial control to an appointed board, not elected officials, and arguing against the mandatory annual levy.

The board wrote a response and sent it to the newspapers to publish, noting their success in bringing Olmsted to Seattle and touting the benefit "every section of the city" would gain from the plan's implementation. They defended setting a minimum levy rate by explaining it would keep park development steady, not stopping and starting with the inevitable fluctuations in the economy. The commissioners also cited the wide public support they had, noting that they had been able to collect 3,000 signatures in support of the amendment, with many of the signers being significant property owners who would be most affected financially by the annual levies.

In the end, the amendment barely passed with a 120-vote majority—3,852 in favor to 3,732 opposed. It provided for a five-member, unsalaried commission, with each commissioner appointed by the mayor and approved by the council for three-year terms. The board would manage all parks employees and could appoint park police to patrol

Charles Saunders, shown here in 1903, worked with Olmsted and the Olmsted Brothers associates from the start of their work until the 1930s, even making a trip to Brookline, Massachusetts, to visit the firm's office in 1905.

John W. Thompson

Remembered by *The Seattle Times* as the "man who abolished the 'Keep Off the Grass' signs in Seattle Parks, Thompson shaped the city's park system as the park superintendent from 1904 until 1921. Prior to his arrival in Seattle, he had worked with the Olmsted Brothers in Louisville, Kentucky, and Watertown, New York. In recommending him to the park board, Olmsted wrote that he was good at executing plans and managing men. Olmsted also wrote that Thompson was not interested in the "statistical and literary side of park work, but he is one of the most practical men with whom we have had to do in our work." After his abrupt departure from Seattle's park department in 1921, Thompson moved to Sumner, Washington, and opened a nursery business. By the time of his death in 1937, he had returned to Seattle to live with his daughter.

John W. Thompson (far right) with Jefferson Park Golf Course officials, 1913.

park properties. The city council retained power of approval over the commissioners' annual budget and over parkland designations and acquisitions. The amendment provided for Park Department funding with 10 percent of the city's revenue from fines, fees, and licenses, and from rents or other revenue from parklands, appropriations made by the city council, and the annual levy. The new park board was made up of the existing commissioners: Charles E. Fowler, J. Edward Shrewsbury, Charles W. Saunders, Elbert F. Blaine, and Melody Choir. Choir's term expired on May 1 and he was replaced by Charles H. Clarke, a grocery distributor with the Kelley-Clarke Company.

Over the next year, the park board turned to Olmsted repeatedly for advice and assistance in getting the Park Department in working order and to establish policies. First, in order to circumvent civil service rules requiring an open application process, the park board asked Olmsted to help them hire a superintendent through his firm. Olmsted agreed to help Seattle find a suitable candidate and pay him for one year, provided that the firm was also hired for park work. An unsigned letter, likely written by Olmsted, recommended three candidates with whom he had worked. One of them was John W. Thompson, of Watertown, New York, who had helped implement their plan for Iroquois Park in Louisville, Kentucky. The firm had brought him to Watertown when their work there began in 1900.

Because of funding challenges, work had stalled on Watertown Park, and Olmsted thought a hiatus for Thompson from that work to implement the Seattle plan would be advantageous for both parties.

Thompson arrived in Seattle in early May 1904 and got settled at the "old Phinney homestead" house in Woodland Park. He toured the existing parks with the park commissioners and then met with Mayor Richard A. Ballinger and park board president Fowler. *The Seattle Times* reported that Thompson expected the park system implementation to take five years. In reality, he would remain in the role for nearly two decades and be a key part of the park system's development.

A second issue arose in early June 1904, when Charles P. Dose offered to donate parkland on Lake Washington, but with several strings attached. The park board sought Olmsted's advice and he replied, "No land should be accepted . . . on any condition requiring the expenditure of public funds in improving and maintaining it without a deed conveying the land to the city for park purposes

Phinney homestead house, 1891. It would become part of Woodland Park when the city bought the property from the Estate of Guy Phinney. John W. Thompson lived here temporarily after arriving in Seattle in 1904.

The Olmsted Brothers delivered the first Lincoln Park preliminary plan, also in early June. It was laid out as a landscape park without playground facilities because, Olmsted wrote in the accompanying report, "very decided preferences of the citizens of the locality have instructed us that no provision is to be made in the design for more vigorous forms of play, and particularly the design must be such as to make baseball impracticable." Because of the site's openness and in keeping with the nearby homes "of good class," Olmsted chose a more formal design. He allowed plenty of opportunities for "shortcutting" (paths) across the space because the denser population in the surrounding area would lead to more people passing through the park as they moved between the residential and business districts. To make the lawn unsuitable for baseball, he placed two rows of purple-leaved beech running along an axis aligned with the "conspicuous and attractive" fountain in the city reservoir on the north side of the tract.

Saunders wrote back to Olmsted promptly, informing him of changed attitudes toward playground facilities at Lincoln Park. He reported that the general feeling was in favor of a mix of formal landscape features and recreational facilities. Olmsted sent the revised plan in July. In the accompanying report, he raised concerns about safety around the baseball field. He emphasized the need to limit field use to grammar-school-age boys and encouraged the installation of fences on three sides of the field to prevent park users from wandering into the outfield. He suggested they cover the fences to make them less conspicuous. He made the northern portion of the park more formal and aligned the primary axis of the design with the reservoir's gatehouse. Along the southwest side, he located tennis courts. A pathway circumnavigated the entire park, including the reservoir. A fieldhouse in the middle of the park provided restrooms, and two pergolas extending east and west of the main structure created shady spaces for caregivers watching children. The sand courts, wading pool, and "gymnastic apparatus" lay to the north of the structure, forming the southern edge of a bowl-shaped lawn that sloped up to the reservoir and was bordered by an arc of trees.

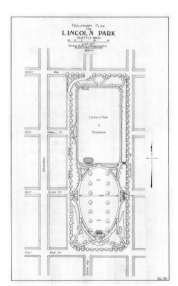

Preliminary Plan for Lincoln Park (Cal Anderson Park), 1904.

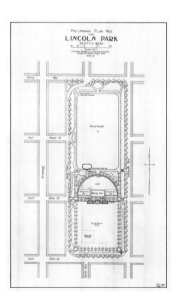

Preliminary Plan No. 2 for Lincoln Park, 1904.

having been previously recorded conveying full title to the City." The board would later accept Dose's donation without restrictions and it would become part of Colman Park.

While the charter amendment process was underway, the park board began implementing the Olmsted plan. In February 1904, they asked the firm to submit a proposal for designing a drive through Washington Park. The park board wanted the roadway to run from Madison Street to the north boundary of the park, with a branch extending westerly from the park to the proposed Interlaken Boulevard and another leading easterly to the Puget Mill Company property on the east side of the park (today's Broadmoor neighborhood). A flurry of letters followed, several crossing each other in transit. In one, Olmsted emphasized that they would, for $200, provide only an alignment for the drive, with no "instructions as to walks, graceful side slopes on the park side of the drives, drainage, planting or other matters of detail, as we assume that without visits to the ground, which would involve too much expense without other adequate employment in Seattle, we should not be able to give advice in these matters of detail efficiently."

In the next letter on the matter, in March 1904, Saunders wrote that the park board had returned to wanting to commission a full park design, but then, finally, in April, they reversed course yet again and asked Olmsted to design only the drive, which would allow them to begin work that summer. Olmsted replied, "We wish to say again that the attempt to plan a small section of a park is bound to be a very unsatisfactory thing to us and were it not that you hold out the hope that before long your board will modify the agreement with us by ordering at least general plans covering the whole of Washington and Woodland parks we should have felt disposed to decline to supply plans for a part of them only." (The park board had also contacted Olmsted regarding a partial plan for Woodland Park.)

Washington Park, 1904.

There appears to have been some board intrigue involved in the discussion about Washington Park. Board president Fowler wrote Olmsted a confidential letter in mid-April explaining that he and Saunders were trying to rein in Blaine, who did not see a need to hire the firm to design the drive or advise on underbrush clearing in the park. Blaine was a Democrat and, with the recent election of a Republican mayor, Fowler believed he would be replaced with a new appointee. Olmsted replied that planning a portion of a park was far from ideal, but they would accommodate the park board's wishes and hope the commission would be expanded to cover the entire park very soon.

Olmsted raised concerns about the board's piecemeal approach in a separate letter to Saunders in September 1904. He was also frustrated that the commissioners continued to ask for advice without being willing to hire the firm for system-wide consultation. This put them in an awkward position and, more importantly, he explained,

it is very unreasonable that we should be limited in our employment. . . . The design for a park must necessarily be in its main features considered as a unit. A design that would be suitable for a 20-acre tract would almost be entirely unsuitable for a 100-acre tract. Practically we cannot make a design for the 20-acre tract in Woodland Park without considering the design of the whole park. There is a difference, it is true, between a preliminary general plan and the detailed plans and advice which we have agreed to furnish. Our claim, therefore, is that we ought to be employed for at least a general plan for these two parks at one price and, if your Board is unwilling to have us prepare grading and other detailed plans for the whole park, our compensation for these detailed plans for a portion of the park should be in addition to our fee for the general plan for the whole park.

And in relation to Washington Park, he wrote, "The drive is not the primary purpose of the park. The park is a piece of landscape or series of landscapes and the drive is merely the means of making those landscapes conveniently accessible and enjoyable by people in carriages and on foot." They appealed to Saunders specifically because, "You know, as an architect, that it would be unreasonable for the city to ask you to prepare a design and working drawings for a portion about 30- or 40-feet square of a proposed new city hall."

The park board did not answer Olmsted's letter directly, possibly because they had no funding to develop Washington Park beyond the drive. Further, because the park board already owned all the land involved in the project, the drive could be developed without having to acquire more land or deal with subdivision plats or private landowners. It was the quickest option for demonstrating what the park and parkway system could achieve. The Olmsted Brothers developed a plan for the Washington Park drive, and the park board accepted it in August 1904. James Frederick Dawson, Olmsted's associate, arrived shortly thereafter to inspect the work underway and provide advice. Dawson would work closely with Thompson during numerous trips to Seattle over the next decade to carry out Olmsted's vision for the park system and in the various landscapes.

James Frederick Dawson

James Frederick Dawson, familiarly known as Fred Dawson, was born in 1874. His family lived at Harvard University's Arnold Arboretum, where his father served as the head plantsman and superintendent. Dawson graduated from the Bussey Institute at Harvard University, which was associated with the arboretum. He began as an apprentice landscape architect with the Olmsted Brothers firm in 1896. He worked alongside John and Rick Olmsted for many years and served as the firm's representative on a number of West Coast projects. He met his future wife, Hazel Belle Lease, while working in Spokane. He visited Washington a number of times after John Olmsted's death in 1920 and corresponded regularly with several of the firm's clients. One of those clients, Sophie Krauss, would be key to his being commissioned in 1934 for his last project in Seattle, the Washington Park Arboretum. When he died in 1941, *The Seattle Times* described him as "the man who had more than any other to do in planning to make Seattle a beautiful city."

From left to right, Fred Dawson, Rick Olmsted, and Percy Gallagher consulting a landscape plan, 1934.

That winter, in January 1905, the park board designated a two-block tract at 16th Avenue and Washington Street for the system's first playground. The Hill Tract, as it was known (later renamed Collins Playfield, it is now the site of the private Wisteria Park), was in the vicinity of one of the playgrounds recommended in the 1903 plan. The surrounding area, now known as the Central District, was a developing neighborhood at the time. The city council authorized its purchase but, at Olmsted's suggestion, it was not fully developed until 1907, in order to put as much money as possible toward land acquisition.

In Spring 1905, the park board sought Olmsted's advice on a proposed ordinance related to regulation of street trees. The parking strips—the portion of street rights-of-way dedicated to landscaping—fell into a gray area between the Department of Streets and the Park Department. Olmsted advised that the park board have jurisdiction because the Park Department would have space for a tree nursery and would be able to supply, plant correctly, and maintain street trees. Also, the Park Department would have a landscape architect who could ensure the plantings were well designed. Ideally, he wrote, a city forester would be added to the department's staff to manage the parking strips. This issue would come up again later, but the parking strips would not be put under the jurisdiction of the park board, except for those in park boulevard rights-of-way.

One other project undertaken in the first year of implementation did not go as smoothly as the park planning. In April 1905, the park board threw up its hands in frustration with City Engineer Thomson and the Engineering Department when Thomson proved to be "brusque and almost insulting" when consulting with the commissioners about Interlaken Boulevard. The engineers had actively worked against park board plans during the previous months, providing shoddy surveys that slowed work and routing a sewage line into the brook that flowed through Washington Park, effectively ruining it. Instead of continuing to work with Thomson to lay out Interlaken Boulevard, the park board hired George Cotterill, who was then in private practice. Acquiring the land for a route all the way to Volunteer Park proved difficult because George Kinnear had platted his parcel in the area, causing land prices to go up. Instead of sweeping around the north side of Capitol Hill, Cotterill decided to zigzag up the hill from a midpoint on Washington Park's western boundary to 19th Avenue East near East Galer Street. From there it would follow 19th Avenue East and East Highland Drive to Volunteer Park.

In March 1905, a committee from the school board came before the park board to discuss school playgrounds. They wanted the park board to help develop and manage school playgrounds. The park board declined to take responsibility for those playgrounds directly adjacent to schools and intended primarily for student use, but offered to supply plants for use in schoolyards. The issue of playgrounds—with equipment, ballfields, and other facilities for children's play—would arise repeatedly over the coming years as the national playground movement gained in popularity. Olmsted agreed with the need to provide such facilities, but felt strongly that the park

Playground adjacent to Ravenna School, located at NE 68th Street and Ravenna Avenue NE.

board should not own or manage parks designed only for athletics. Instead, he would argue that playgrounds (or playfields, with facilities for older children) under the park board's jurisdiction should be designed as parks first, with the equipment and fields integrated into a park setting, while facilities intended primarily to serve children during school hours, without park features such as lawns, paths, and planting beds, belonged under the school board's jurisdiction.

Before the park board could do much more toward realizing Olmsted's plan, they needed to raise funds for land acquisition. The provisions of the charter amendment allowed the park board to send a request to the city council to place a measure on the ballot for voters to approve an additional property tax

Plan for Boulevard in Washington Park

The boulevard plan for Washington Park featured several hallmarks of an Olmsted design. It curved gently and gracefully along the valley, with a walk running parallel to it. Although the commission included only the roadway, Olmsted and his associate Percy Jones looked at the park's topography and existing forest and made notes about the vistas that could be experienced as visitors moved along the boulevard, where views could be opened up, and how the future park might be laid out.

Based on his initial studies of desired sightlines, Olmsted developed a planting plan in 1905 for the shrubs, trees, and lawns that would flank the drive. Alongside the 24-foot driveway there was provision for an 8-foot sidewalk that followed as near to the roadway as the contours allowed, crossing from time to time as needed. Alongside the boulevard, the plantings included individual species of trees in informal groupings and large shrub beds, with small trees behind them. In keeping with its park surroundings, the plantings along the drive were informal and included many native species. When Olmsted sent the boulevard plans to the Board of Park Commissioners, he wrote: "In our list of plants you will note that we have not used a great many of the plants listed in your nursery. We found that you have many plants of a formal or exotic nature well adapted to use in city squares and small parks, but not so well suited for larger and less artificial work." For the south entry from Madison Street, Olmsted planned a more formal planting of oak and sycamore trees along the drive. These same trees frame the park entrance today.

The view south from Interlaken Boulevard as it joins Lake Washington Boulevard in Washington Park, 1911.

Volunteer Park Preliminary Plans

The Olmsted Brothers submitted their preliminary plan for Volunteer Park in September 1904. Although called a preliminary plan, it was a general plan for the entire park intended to guide future work. For Volunteer Park, the firm would be hired to plan and guide work over a number of years, leading to the development of grading plans, planting plans, architectural drawings, and other guidance. It would be the most formal park design in the system, in keeping with its central location in a residential neighborhood.

The Olmsted plan reserved most of the eastern side of the park and the upper portion of the western side north of the reservoir for greenswards (large open lawns with trees and planting beds at the edges). The far western edge of the park was planted with trees interspersed with open areas.

A concourse following along the ridge formed the north-south axis, and the east-west axis aligned with the existing city reservoir, which Olmsted incorporated into his design to take advantage of the reflective qualities of the water and western

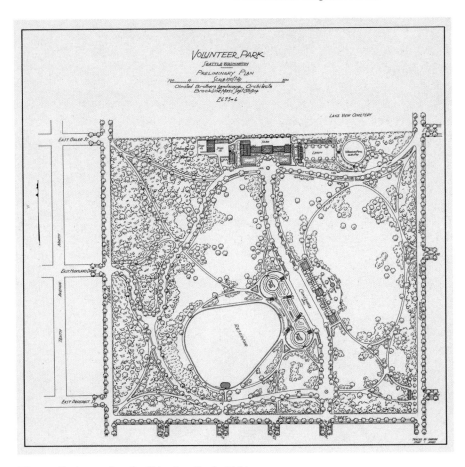

First preliminary plan for Volunteer Park, 1904.

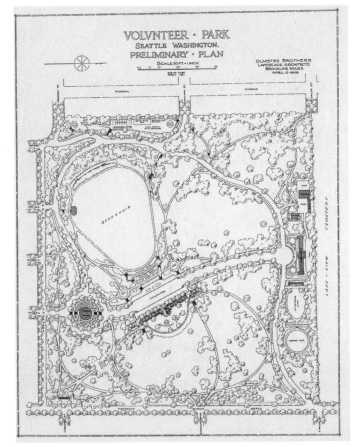

Revised preliminary plan for Volunteer Park, 1909.

views provided over its surface. A carriage drive created a drive through the western portion of the park. From the northern end of the concourse, it curved down to the west, across the base of the ravine, into which the reservoir had been built in 1901, then turned east to rejoin the concourse at its southern end. Pathways curved gracefully through each side of the park. To buffer the park from the cemetery that lay to the north, Olmsted located a "little folks lawn," a wading pool, a shelterhouse, a conservatory, and the park's greenhouses and work yard along the northern border. Along the east side of the concourse, across from the reservoir, Olmsted placed a pergola with a concert grove and a simple bandstand. On the west side of the concourse, a planting area extended down the slope to the reservoir path. This formal planting area was bracketed by a lily pool at either end.

While Thompson began some preliminary work on the planting beds, guided by the preliminary plan, the Water Department began preparations to build a standpipe in Volunteer Park. Seattle's public water system is gravity-fed, meaning the pressure of the water moving downhill from the Cedar River watershed in the Cascade Mountains pushes it through pipes and into the city reservoirs. From the reservoirs, the water flows downhill into surrounding homes and businesses. A water tower is needed to provide sufficient water pressure to those businesses and homes built at the same or higher elevation as the reservoir on top of Capitol Hill. Olmsted saw the standpipe as an opportunity to provide an observatory that would afford views across the city. In December 1905, Olmsted wrote that the standpipe would be a "large and conspicuous artificial object which is apparently intended to project upward from a circular mound," so it should be sited "to have an agreeable sense of relation to other formal improvements in its neighborhood." He recommended a location 300

View north from the Volunteer Park water tower in 1913 showing the recently completed concourse, concert grove, and pergola, with the conservatory in the background.

feet from the center of Prospect Street, aligned with 14th Avenue East and the concourse, which would encircle it.

In 1909 the park board asked for a revised preliminary plan for the park. Olmsted incorporated new vehicular entrances at 11th and 12th Avenues and East Prospect Street and a playground for older children in the southwest corner of the park. This plan would be implemented (with the playground relocated to the northeast corner) and was largely completed by 1912.

Brochure published in about 1911 to promote Seattle's public parks, playgrounds, and boulevards, which "will be an important factor in making Seattle famous."

levy for acquisitions. The council could then decide if it was willing to allocate that amount of the city's allowed indebtedness to Park Department funding. The park board decided to ask for a $500,000 park bond measure, to be placed on the December 1905 special election ballot.

The city council agreed, and the park board began working in tandem with the newspapers to get public support for the measure. A *Seattle Times* editorial in October emphasized the value of investing in parks, stating, "We believe that every dollar expended along the lines indicated will return five dollars in actual [land] values to the City of Seattle within a decade." *The Seattle Star* ran an editorial by park board president C. J. Smith defending the somewhat unusual request to approve the bond measure without an explicit delineation of what property would be purchased because, he wrote, "We cannot afford to be made the victims of real estate sharks by showing our hand previous to making purchases." To avoid those speculators who would take advantage of any specific information, they referred voters to the 1903 plan for a general sense of how the funds would be spent.

The chair of the city council's committee on streets, Frank P. Mullen, fired back in a separate editorial in *The Seattle Star*. He criticized Interlaken Boulevard and questioned whether the Board of Park Commissioners should be entrusted with $500,000. He thought the acquisition of additional property unnecessary, that the planned parkways only really served people who had "fast horses," or automobiles (still a very small number), and that the arrangement invited graft. Further, the city already had significant

debt, and Mullen did not approve of adding to that burden.

Smith responded in yet another editorial that there remained plenty of debt capacity for the city to fund improvements to electricity or water systems, or to other infrastructure. He countered the argument against property acquisition by citing the rapid increase in property values seen throughout the city. As they had found with Interlaken Boulevard, the land needed for development of the Olmsted plan would only get significantly and rapidly more expensive. Smith rejected the claim that parkways were of limited utility, reminding readers that each parkway would have walkways, bridle trails, bicycle paths, and vehicular traffic lanes. He reassured the public that the park board would "follow exactly the recommendations of Mr. Olmsted. We expect to be besieged with a host of land owners, each with his little axe to grind, but we will not deviate a hairsbreadth from the plans recommended by an expert of national reputation."

Just before the December vote, *The Seattle Times* ran an editorial that quoted President Theodore Roosevelt's recent message to Congress extolling the benefits of public parks and warning, "For a happy-go-lucky lack of concern for the youth of today, the community will have to pay a terrible penalty of financial burden and social degradation tomorrow. . . . Public playgrounds are necessary means for the development of wholesome citizenship in modern cities." Despite that warning and the park commissioners' public relations efforts, the park bond failed by a narrow margin on December 28, 1905. The yea votes outnumbered the nays, but bond

Park playgrounds, like this one in Roanoke Park in 1910, were often discussed, but it took some time to realize them.

measures required at least three-fifths of the registered voters to cast votes, and voter participation did not meet that threshold.

Undeterred, the Board of Park Commissioners sent a new request to the council on January 2, 1906. The board felt that placing the measure on a special election ballot had put it at a disadvantage. The next election, scheduled for March 1906, would be a general election for city offices and attract more voters because of the higher-profile contests. As part of the new campaign, Commissioner Blaine wrote an article for *The Seattle Times* about his views on the park system. He recounted his recent trip to the East Coast by train. After visiting parks in midwestern and eastern cities, including a tour of Boston's parks with John Olmsted, he returned by train. Describing his return to Seattle, he wrote,

> *As I reached the shores of Puget Sound and again viewed its placid waters, its magnificent mountains and towering peaks, I said to myself that here is the*

grandest and the most majestic scenery, and the choicest spot of all in which to dwell. Firmer than ever am I of the opinion that the Pacific Coast and notably Puget Sound, for the next fifty years, is going to be one of the theatres of our country's greatest activity.

He warned that if Seattle did not develop its parks and make the city more attractive, people would only stay long enough to make their fortunes before moving to more beautiful cities. Further, he urged that the park system be built to provide an alternative to saloons and gambling because "No human being who keeps in close touch with nature can become despondent."

The editorials and letters from commissioners repeatedly emphasized that the bond funds would be used for acquisitions, not park improvements. They warned that if they were delayed in buying land, the city would pay much higher prices or not be able to acquire the needed land at all. Once parcels were developed for residential or commercial uses, they would no longer be available for parks. While this was a very real concern as the city's population continued to grow rapidly, on its way to 237,000 people in 1910, it may have also been an effort to answer criticisms about *where* land was being acquired. Some improvement clubs believed other areas were getting disproportionate investments in their parks. The north end's clubs particularly complained about the amount of work being done in Washington Park while Woodland Park saw hardly any investment.

The election on March 6, 1906, had enough voter participation to be valid, and the park bond measure received a majority of votes. The same north end wards that had been tepid supporters in the first vote

saw the most opposition, but only one actually voted it down with a majority. It was noted that these were the same wards that would benefit the most from the bond measure's passage, but voters apparently were still skeptical about the park plan and its costs or the Board of Park Commissioners' execution of it. With the passage of the bond measure, the park board could begin in earnest to acquire the land identified in the "reduced plan" in Olmsted's 1903 report.

Work commenced on extending the main pleasure drive in April 1906. The park board hired George Cotterill to lay out the drive extending north from Washington Park to the university campus and south from the park toward Lake Washington. Both extensions would run into issues with property acquisition as the parkway crossed through existing subdivisions. On the north, Cotterill would also have to adjust the drive to accommodate the Army Corps of Engineers' relocation of the Lake Washington Ship Canal from the already-platted southern route across the Montlake isthmus to a new northern route in December 1907.

Completing a connection between Washington Park and the university campus grew more urgent in June 1906, when the Alaska-Yukon-Pacific Exposition Company, in charge of planning the 1909 world's fair in Seattle, chose the campus for its grounds. Since attracting new residents and businesses to the city and surrounding region was the primary reason for holding the exposition, the fair organizers wanted Seattle to look its best, while the park board also wanted to take advantage of the wave of investment being made in the city to further the park system's development.

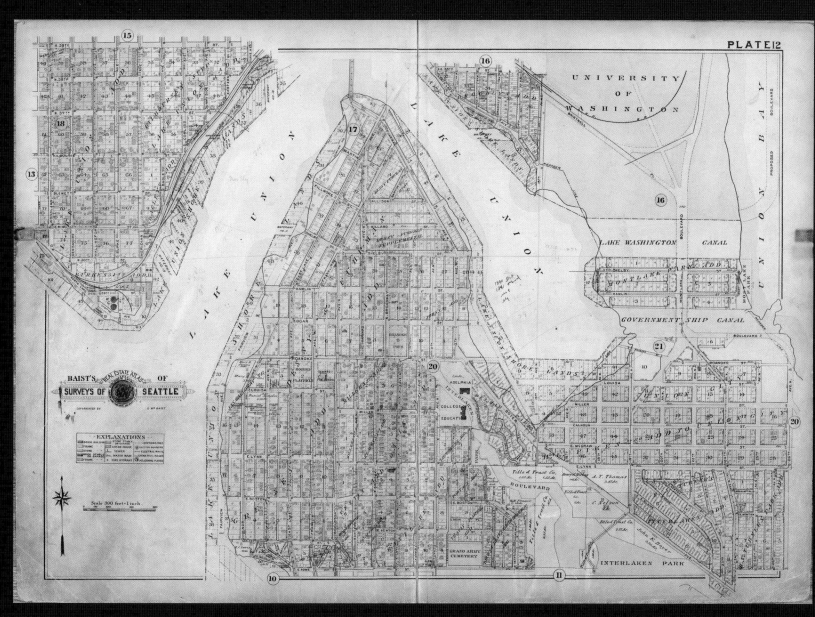

1912 Baist Real Estate Map showing the Montlake isthmus with the early canal reserve on the south and the actual right-of-way for the Lake Washington Ship Canal cut between Lake Washington and Lake Union on the north. The park on the east side of the Montlake Park Addition would be enlarged when the cut opened and Lake Washington was lowered by about nine feet in 1916.

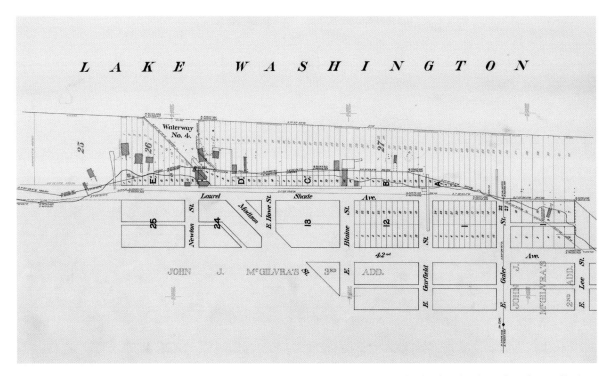

Shorelands along the Madison Park neighborhood (marked in green). The state sold the shorelands within the city limits (from Union Bay to Hanford Street) to provide funding for the Alaska-Yukon-Pacific Exposition.

Further south, along Lake Washington, the Hunter Tract Improvement Company approached the park board in September 1906 with an offer to sell land for a park and shoreline boulevard adjacent to their subdivision. Daniel Jones, the former park board president, and Fred L. Fehren, along with some adjacent landowners, were developing the Hunter Tract, as it was then known, for large homes in a parklike neighborhood they named Mount Baker for its views of the distant mountain. George Cotterill, who was laying out the plan, and Jones consulted with Olmsted on his October 1906 visit to Seattle. Cotterill showed Olmsted the draft of his plan and they discussed the road alignments and the shoreline.

The plan reserved land for a park (if the park board decided to buy it) extending up the saddle in the hill from the lakeshore and a curving parkway running from McClellan Street to 30th Avenue. It also included a short stretch of boulevard south of South Hanford Street (now named Hunter Boulevard) and four very small parks sited among the residential lots. Olmsted wrote to Daniel Jones that

it will certainly be to your credit in respect to liberal treatment of the public in park matters, as well as in providing for future residents lands to be used in common, and in which the remarkably beautiful views of and across Lake Washington . . . can be enjoyed. The topography of the land is such that even after houses are built on all the lots there will be more or less opportunity for glimpses of the mountains, from each of them, yet anyone will enjoy still more an occasional stroll through the lands that are to be dedicated to park purposes, so as to obtain other and different views amid natural surrounds. Undoubtedly setting aside some of the land for park purposes will enhance the market value of all the lots.

Along the shoreline, the developers wanted the city to acquire the adjacent 75 feet of underwater shoreland for the lakeshore parkway and agree to extend the upland boulevard (today's Mount Baker Boulevard) from 30th Avenue South to Rainier Avenue South. The shorelands were an issue because it was believed the Army Corps of Engineers would build one set of locks at Ballard for the Lake Washington Ship Canal, which would require lowering Lake Washington by about 10 feet, to bring it down to the level of Lake Union. The state would then sell the newly exposed land, possibly to the highest bidder, without regard for the adjacent landowners. If the city preemptively acquired the shoreland for park uses, it would protect it from being used for commercial or low-value residential structures.

In a November 1906 letter to park board president J. Edward Shrewsbury, Olmsted suggested the city pursue state legislation to donate all publicly owned shorelands to the city for park purposes. When the legislature convened in January 1907, State Senator George Piper introduced a bill pertaining to shoreland sales. It incorporated a provision related to Olmsted's recommendation, allowing any shoreland lying adjacent to city-owned land to be automatically transferred to the city, at no cost. The rest of the shorelands would be sold to fund the permanent

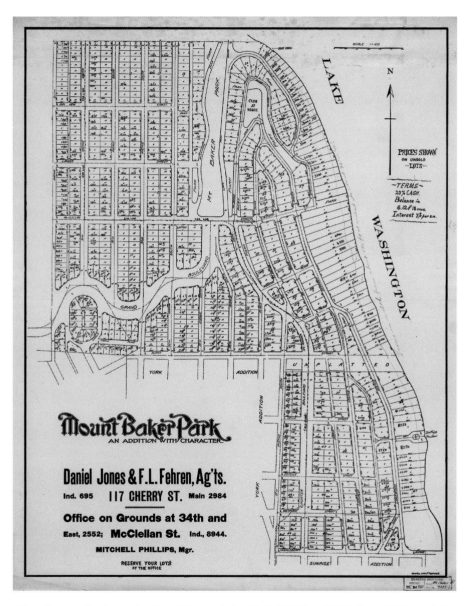

Advertisement for the newly platted Mount Baker Park Addition, 1907. Notes, likely made by Olmsted, and a hand-drawn line show the area along the lakeshore that would be donated to the city for park use to ensure that the adjoining shorelands would be transferred to the City of Seattle under the terms of the shorelands sale bill passed that year by the state legislature.

buildings at the Alaska-Yukon-Pacific Exposition. These were the buildings that would be used by the university after the world's fair. A small dustup ensued when it became apparent that some property owners planned to donate small strips of land, perhaps as small as one-foot wide, to prevent the sale of the adjacent shorelands. If too many people did this, the exposition funding would fall short. When asked by commissioner C. J. Smith about the conflict of interest, Olmsted replied that, since transferring ownership of the shorelands to the city was consistent with the 1903 plan, it was "eminently proper and very

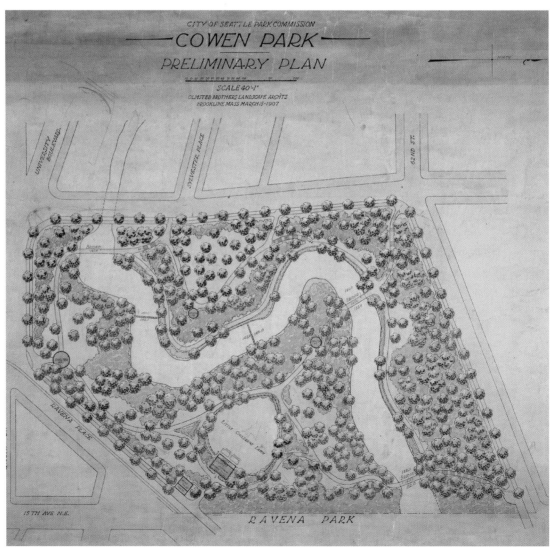

Preliminary plan for Cowen Park, 1907.

fortunate." Further, he continued, "the park interests of the City were permanent and would ever be most important and that of the two it was certainly best to sacrifice the Exposition," if the state would not make up any deficit that might result from the donations.

By the end of 1906, the park system had grown considerably with donations from property owners and purchases. The family of the recently deceased Pendleton Miller donated a tract of land for a new playground in his memory. They wrote to the park board, "We wish to offer to donate to the City of Seattle the land lying between 19th and 20th Avenues and East Thomas and East Harrison Streets, for a public playground, to be known as the 'Pendleton Miller Playground.' This we do in memory of our beloved son and brother who ever enjoyed seeing children in outdoor play, and who with zest and manliness entered the field of sport." The land would later be swapped for a nearby two-block parcel that was more conveniently located for students of Longfellow School (now Edmond S. Meany Middle School). In June, the park board agreed to purchase half of the land needed for a playground adjacent to B. F. Day School in Fremont. The city vacated the existing street between the two parcels to facilitate the playground's development and use.

In the north end, private developers propelled the park system's development forward with two projects not anticipated by Olmsted in 1903 but in keeping with his intentions for the park system. In June 1906, Charles Cowen offered to sell the park board a tract of land adjacent to Ravenna Park, which was still privately owned. Cowen wanted the park developed as part of his recently platted Cowen's University

Footbridge crossing a creek in Cowen Park.

Park Addition. The plat also held open a couple of blocks around the brook that lay along the boulevard route Olmsted had identified between Ravenna Park and Green Lake. In October, having realized the city would not buy the park lots, Cowen decided instead to donate the land. The park board named the park in Cowen's honor and wrote in their acknowledgment that the gift, "from one almost a stranger in our midst, an alien by birth [he had immigrated to the United States from England], carries with it a sentiment not often expressed. No gift given to the city, through our board, has given us greater encouragement in our work and endeavors to make Seattle beautiful, than that of Mr. Cowen's."

To the south of Cowen Park, James Moore platted his University Park Addition in 1906. Located north of NE 45th Street and east of 15th Avenue NE, the plat included a broad boulevard with a wide median running from 45th Street to NE Ravenna Boulevard. While it was not a direct realization of the 1903 plan

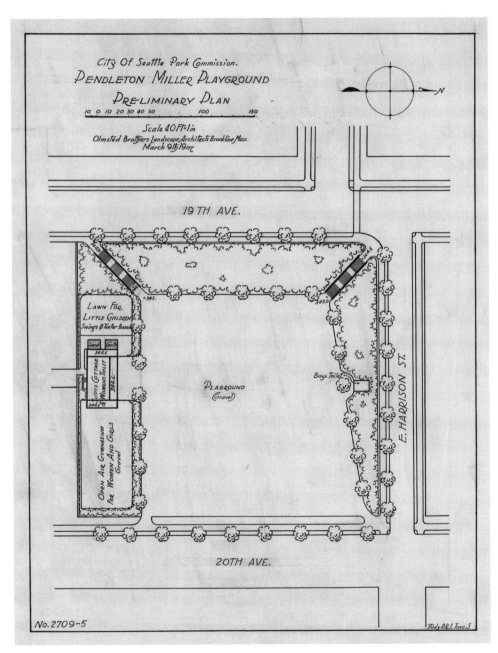

Preliminary plan for Pendleton Miller Playground, 1907.

for a connection between the university and Ravenna Park, and not curvilinear like an ideal Olmstedian boulevard, Moore intended it to be a link in the chain of parks and parkways and advertised University Boulevard (actually 17th Avenue NE) as part of the Olmsted park system. Later developments with Montlake Boulevard would provide a more direct connection between Lake Washington Boulevard and Ravenna Boulevard, but University Boulevard provided a link between the campus and Ravenna Boulevard, and the park board would designate it as part of the system in 1909.

Not long after the Cowen donation in October 1906, park commissioner John M. Frink and his wife, Abbie H. Frink, donated to the city land they owned in the Rainier Heights neighborhood (the Leschi Park area today). The parcel lay just south of Leschi Park (owned by the Seattle Electric Company) and encompassed a portion of the land Olmsted referred to in his 1903 report as the more rugged and steep portion of the landslide area, which he believed should be only minimally developed. The park would be named Frink Park in the family's honor.

The Board of Park Commissioners hired the Olmsted Brothers to design plans for both Cowen and Frink Parks, as well as Miller Playfield, and the University Extension, which referred to the drive between Washington Park and the university campus. Olmsted wrote a letter to Shrewsbury once he had formulated ideas for each landscape, so the park board could get a sense of where his plans were headed and give him any suggestions they might have. The letter provides insight into Olmsted's thoughts on the park board's progress on the park system three years after it was designed and gave the commissioners guidance on the next steps they should take.

Overall, Olmsted's letter conveyed satisfaction. He wrote, "I will take this occasion to say that I am much gratified by the progress that has been made in the development of the Park System since my report on the comprehensive system." He commented that the money invested thus far had been well spent and advised that it was time to put some toward improving (not just acquiring) playgrounds. He urged the park commissioners to resist public pressure for acquiring small parks and playgrounds scattered about the city and focus on acquiring the large parks identified in the system plan. He feared that if they delayed, the forested tracts within reach of a "five cent [street] car fare" (which would have been the distance from downtown to the outer edges of urban development at that time) would be logged before they could be acquired.

Olmsted continued his letter with a prioritized list of steps the board should take next. First, they should extend Washington Park to the university campus along the shore of Union Bay, including Foster Island, before it was taken for industrial or residential uses. Next, they should acquire the right-of-way for the parkway between Cowen Park and Green Lake, including the "brook and its bushy banks" and enough level land to build playgrounds and ballfields along its length. On the southeast side of town, Olmsted noted that the park system was "very deficient." He felt that the price being asked for Mount Baker Park was reasonable. Likewise, he warned that the price of Bailey Peninsula (Seward Park today) would only remain reasonable until the streetcar line reached it.

Looking more broadly at the system, Olmsted gave some general recommendations. He reiterated the need to acquire parkland, "mainly upon areas along the shore of Lake Washington, including also an area on Magnolia Bluffs overlooking the Sound." Out of concern for the park board's budget, Olmsted warned that acquiring too many more playgrounds, with their higher development costs, would be "short-sighted." This was particularly because he did not "think the city is yet so large and the working population so crowded as to make it so vitally essential to provide play grounds in the midst of the dense population as it is in cities of two or three times the population of Seattle." Unlike many Eastern cities, Seattle still had some elbow room.

Olmsted continued his letter with short descriptions of the park designs he was preparing. He discussed his ideas on minimally developing Frink Park's "romantic and secluded ravine and steep wood hillsides" and the "magnificent outlook" at the end of Jackson Street, on the western edge of the park. He offered a couple of strategies for extending the park to the shore of the lake and vacating surrounding city streets. In Cowen Park, Olmsted recommended very few changes. Beyond seeding lawns, clearing out some of the stumps, and thinning a few trees, he was hesitant to disturb the forested ravine too much (it would later be filled with excavated material from the construction of Interstate 5). To make the brook more prominent, he thought the park board might consider asking Ravenna Park's owners, the Becks, if the dam they had built to generate electricity could be moved to the border between the two parks and allowed to back up a pond 800 feet into Cowen Park. He debated the loss of so many trees from the flooding versus the

University Boulevard (17th Avenue NE) looking north from NE 50th Street, 1912.

benefit of a more substantial water feature, leaving the decision open for discussion with the park board.

Although the park board had acquired some land on the west side of Washington Park, Olmsted was concerned about the area surrounding the northwest corner, where the University Extension drive would leave the park. He thought that if they did not manage to acquire more land, the drive would be cramped by other city streets and the views from it ruined. He wanted the drive to leave the park at the mouth of the brook and follow the shore of Union Bay. While the inland side could be fronted by houses, he believed all of the land on the water side, including the submerged shorelands, should be part of the parkway. When the lake was lowered, then the parkland would increase substantially and the drive would grow into a park wrapping around the bay to the campus.

Olmsted finished his letter with comments on the two new playgrounds, Pendleton Miller and the Hill Tract (Collins Playfield). The discussion centered on the intended users—small children and elementary school–aged children—and grading plans, structures such as shelterhouses, and playground equipment. Olmsted emphasized the need for open lawns for children to play upon, and plantings, pathways, and other elements to make the playgrounds aesthetically pleasing.

The discussion about playgrounds was held against the backdrop of the wider playground movement that was surging across the country in 1906. That year, the Playground Association of America formed and held a conference in Washington, D.C. Like other strands of the Progressive movement, the playground advocates used the social sciences to build support for their cause. Proponents argued that

public playgrounds were needed for social and moral development, particularly for immigrant and working-class children.

In Seattle, playgrounds had been on the park board's agenda since before Olmsted's 1903 plan, but a distinct upsurge in appeals to the commissioners to accelerate playground development began in March 1906. Over about two months, several different groups contacted the park board. Members of the Women's Century Club came to the March 15 meeting, along with school board members Ebenezer Shorrock and Ellwood C. Hughes, to discuss playgrounds. They shared information on what Los Angeles' and Chicago's park commissioners were doing. At the next meeting, representatives of the University Heights parents club requested new playground development in the Brooklyn and Latona neighborhoods. The Green Lake Improvement Club inquired about playgrounds planned for that district. It is noteworthy that the women representing these groups are the first to appear in the public record relative to the park system's development. This is likely because of the playgrounds' association with children's development, which was considered part of women's sphere in the gendered division of public life in that era.

In March 1907, representatives from the Seattle Federation of Women's Clubs came before the park board to ask for more playground development. The commissioners agreed they were needed, but still did not have the budget that would allow them to acquire parkland according to the Olmsted plan *and* develop playgrounds. The board suggested that the Federation of Women's Clubs could have its members raise funds to develop playgrounds. That would have been a

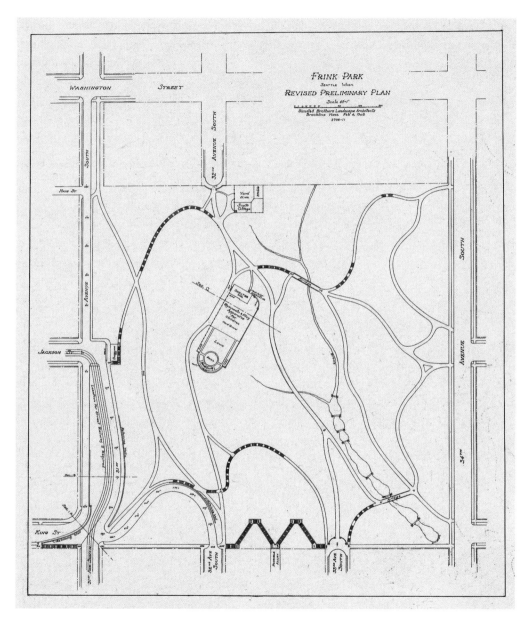

Revised preliminary plan for Frink Park, 1908.

Lake Washington Boulevard bridge across a ravine in Frink Park. It is similar in design to one in The Highlands, an Olmsted-designed neighborhood just north of Seattle. The bridge's railing is also reminiscent of the Nethermead Arches in Brooklyn's Prospect Park.

common activity for women's clubs at that time, but the park board records do not indicate the clubs' response nor any influx of funding for playgrounds from them.

Throughout 1907, preparations for the world's fair continued. In February, the exposition company asked the park board to "loan" them Superintendent Thompson to help Dawson with the plantings for the fair grounds. Dawson had relocated to Seattle to manage the landscape preparations. He grew plants in an on-site nursery, oversaw grading projects, and made sure the trees they wanted to keep stayed in place and the remaining ones were removed. Dawson had a more gregarious personality than Olmsted and formed lasting relationships with Seattleites as he worked on the public projects and the numerous private residential plans the firm was hired to do, including The Highlands subdivision, adjacent to the Seattle Golf Club, located northwest of the city. When the fair opened in 1909, a subhead on a story about the grounds would read, "Wonderful Achievement of Landscape Architect Dawson in Transforming Wilderness into Most Fascinating of Parks."

In May of that year, a conflict erupted over Woodland Park that would presage an issue that has arisen over and over again in the life of the park

The nascent national playground movement gained momentum in the 1900s and playgrounds in Seattle were well-used, as shown in this 1911 photo of Ross Playground.

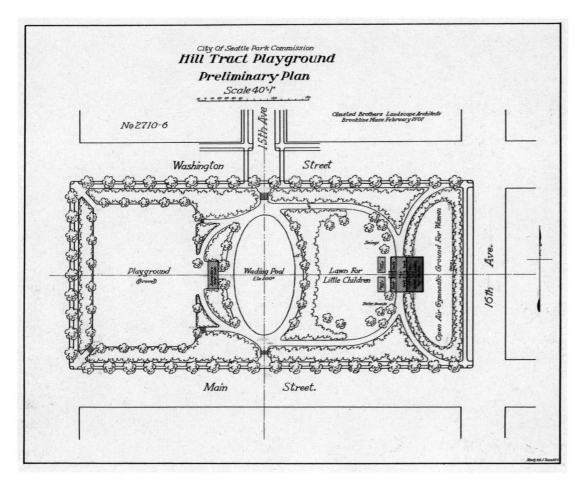

Hill Tract Playground (later Collins Playfield) Preliminary Plan, 1907.

Pamphlet about Seattle playgrounds, published in 1909.

system. The first motor vehicles arrived in Seattle in 1900 and their numbers quickly grew. Vehicle registrations increased from just 327 in King County in 1908 to about 21,000 in 1918. At the same time, more suburban developments emerged at the outer reaches of the city. In the north end, Phinney Ridge's east slope began to fill with homes, and businesses were getting established at what would become the Greenwood neighborhood.

Before long, north end improvement clubs were calling for better roads to connect them with downtown. Seattle's terrain limited the options for routes: steep hills made east-west movement challenging, and waterways, existing and proposed, narrowed the choices for north-south routes. At that time, bridges crossed the waterways at 14th Avenue in Ballard, at Stone Avenue near Fremont, and at Latona, near today's University Bridge. The most direct route

Women from the Washington State and Seattle Federation of Women's Clubs in Longview, Washington, ca. 1925.

from downtown to the north end ran along the east sides of Denny and Queen Anne hills, crossed the lake at Stone Avenue, and then followed that street north to Woodland Park. To get to the other side of the park and Green Lake, City Engineer Thomson proposed carrying a street through the park to the vicinity of Aurora Avenue North and North 65th Street.

The proposed route paralleled the streetcar line through the center of the park. Neighbors protested because the route would cleave the park in two. Initially, the park board did not object, believing the route was in keeping with Olmsted's 1903 plan, as he had mentioned in it that it was likely a "traffic street" would have to be provided across the park and it should "follow one side of the electric railway but need not be wide." A community member, Christopher Horr, wrote to Olmsted after learning that park board president Blaine had referenced him

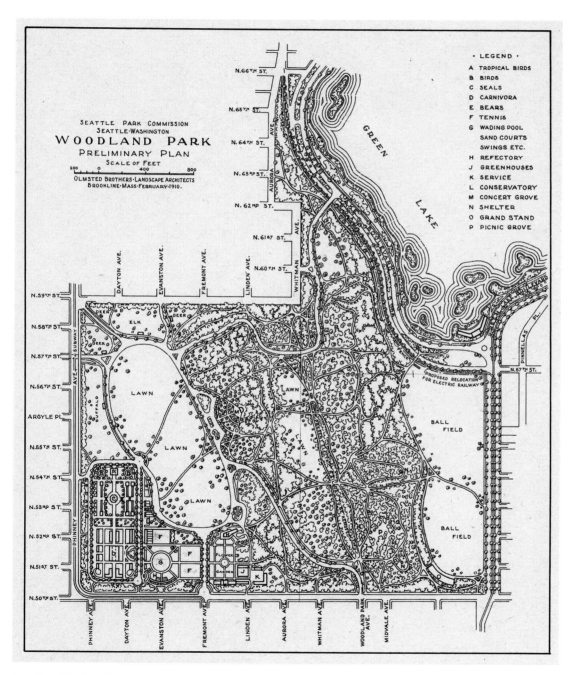

Woodland Park preliminary plan, 1910.

in a discussion over the street extension. Olmsted promptly wrote to Blaine asking that he not cite him in support of the planned route. Blaine replied, explaining that while he had not quoted Olmsted regarding the street alignment, he had understood that Olmsted did not want the street near the shoreline and reminded Olmsted of the 1903 report's recommendation. Blaine believed that growth to the north of the park necessitated a through street, so it needed to be accommodated. Olmsted replied with an offer to take a look at the issue, certain that he could find a more elegant solution than Thomson had.

In early December 1907, the park board requested that Olmsted confer with the Board of Public Works to find a workable solution. Olmsted sent his report to the park board on January 8, 1908. First, he explained,

> One of the most essential landscape features of Woodland Park is the woodland from which it derives its name. To the dwellers in the city, the woodland landscape is one of the most interesting and refreshing sorts as it forms a very complete contrast to all the ordinary city streets and squares and parks. As a matter of practical utility woodlands are very rarely created in public parks and if they exist on lands taken for public parks in the midst of a city, they are almost invariably revolutionized into a very smooth and somewhat unnatural and artificial appearing open grove of trees. In many cases where large numbers of visitors have to be accommodated on a small area, such a treatment of natural woods is entirely reasonable but in cases where the land is very rough and steep, the woods should be left in a more nearly wild condition, that is to say, with the natural undergrowth of shrubbery and wild flowers to be viewed from drives and walks upon which the public may pass without injury to the body of the woods.

With that in mind, he rejected Thomson's suggestion to carry the road through the middle of the park. His first preference would be to carry the drive around the park on its western side, but that was an unlikely outcome due to the length of the detour. In place of that, he preferred a route along the southern lakeshore, with one drive for traffic paralleling a park drive that would connect with the boulevard encircling the lake. Given the amount of traffic that was expected, however, he believed they would also have to build a street along the west side of the streetcar tracks once Woodland Avenue could be widened north and south of the park (it appears that he was referring to Aurora Avenue on the north). Olmsted's thinking appears to have continued to evolve because, in his February 1910 preliminary plan for Woodland Park, there is no indication of the route along the lakeshore being temporary.

The conflict over accommodating city growth while developing the park system indicates how quickly the city was growing during these years. Thousands of people moved to the city each year, and a number of surrounding areas were annexed. South Seattle joined the city in 1905. West Seattle, Ballard,

Study of Fremont Avenue entrance to Woodland Park by Olmsted Brothers draftsman William L. White, 1912.

Columbia City, and South Park voted for annexation to Seattle in 1907. (Georgetown and Laurelhurst were the last to be added in this burst of growth, in 1910.)

The Board of Park Commissioners started receiving requests for parks in the new areas, and questions arose about what lands should be acquired and how they should be acquired. In November 1907 the park board asked Olmsted to provide an informal report on incorporating the newly annexed areas into the park system. He toured the new neighborhoods and met with representatives from the West Seattle, Ballard, Beacon Hill, and Rainier Valley improvement clubs. On December 30, 1907, he made a presentation to the park board, which apparently intrigued them enough to request a formal, written report. Over the next month, Olmsted would work on the plan, extending parkways to knit the city's park system together and locating parks to take advantage of the landscape features and serve the burgeoning residential neighborhoods.

Alaska-Yukon-Pacific Exposition Plan

The Alaska-Yukon-Pacific Exposition Company hired Olmsted to design the world's fair grounds in October 1906. The grounds took up the lower section of campus, away from the existing buildings, giving Olmsted a clean slate upon which he could lay out his plan. The plan he presented in May 1907 incorporated a number of exceptional elements that embody the Olmsted design principles.

Three vistas—Washington, Union, and Rainier—drew the surrounding lakes and mountains into the design. These view corridors extended out from the fountain in the Court of Honor, which ran from the U.S. Government Building, located where Red Square is today, to the Geyser Basin, called Drumheller Fountain today. The Court of Honor featured large, ornate buildings. The structures were temporary, but the grading work done for them and other fair buildings created spaces for the future permanent buildings.

The fair's buildings, paths, and avenues were laid out around the axes created by the vistas. These drew the surrounding landscape into the campus plan, with their views across the water and out to the mountains. A long, more formally designed walk, connected by a series of circles, wrapped around the entire grounds, following the curve of the railroad tracks running through the campus. Smaller, curving paths meandered through the less formal areas.

The planting beds around the buildings, in the Court of Honor, and along Rainier Vista featured thousands of flowering plants, including the cactus dahlia, the official flower of the exposition. Native plants were incorporated into planting plans, such as the Douglas firs that framed the views along each of the vistas. In the lower campus, Olmsted reserved a wooded area on the Lake Washington shore to provide a place of respite from the bustle of the fair, with rustic benches situated for taking in the views across the water.

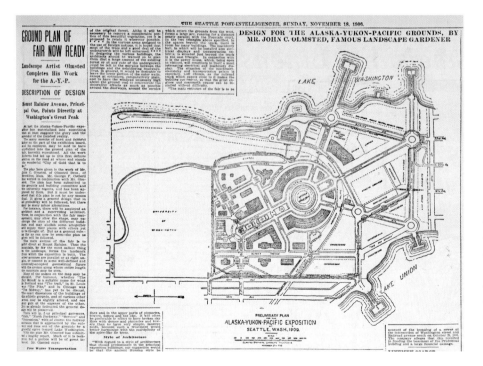

In November 1906 the Seattle Post-Intelligencer *published Olmsted's plan for the Alaska-Yukon-Pacific Exposition, to be held on the University of Washington campus in 1909.*

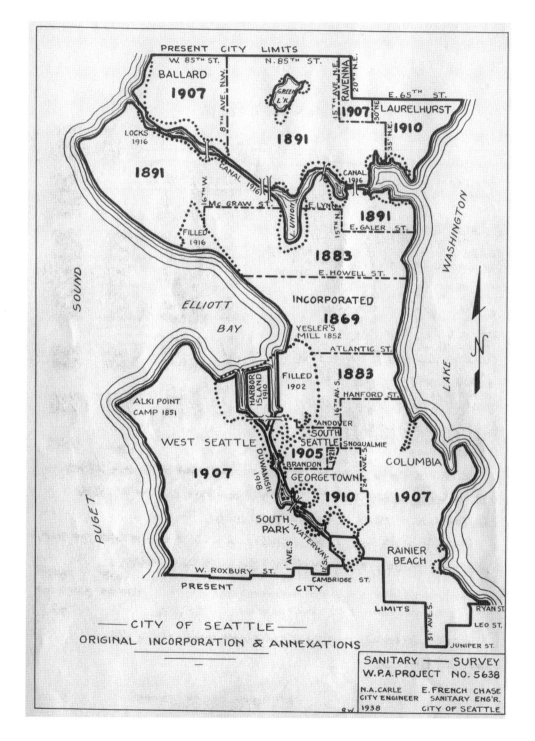

Map showing annexations to Seattle between 1869 and 1910. A burst of annexations between 1906 and 1910 expanded the city's limits to the north, south, and west.

103

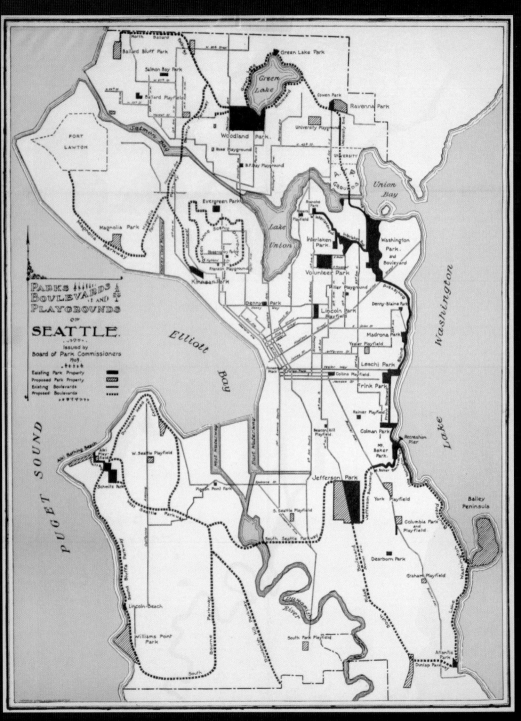

The Board of Park Commissioners issued a special edition of its annual report in 1909 to promote Seattle and its park system to Alaska-Yukon-Pacific Exposition visitors.

CHAPTER 5

GROWING CITY, GROWING PARK SYSTEM

Much of Olmsted's work for Seattle was done without fanfare. In the Olmsted Brothers' correspondence files, a researcher could easily skim past the "Supplemental Report on Annexed Territory and General Development," which Olmsted delivered on January 25, 1908. It is a simple letter, presented without ceremony and never officially adopted by the city council or park board. That belies its significance, which was at least equal to that of the 1903 plan. In it, Olmsted incorporated the newly annexed territories and seamlessly connected them into the existing citywide system so well that it seems as though it might have been his vision all along to have the park system extend to the new areas. The plan laid out in the report would shape the ever-growing city and fill out the parks and boulevards that form the framework of the city's park system today.

The 1908 report differed substantially from the 1903 report. Instead of jumping right into the plan's description as he had in 1903, Olmsted followed the pattern established in park system reports he prepared for other cities, discussing some of the reasoning behind his planning before describing his place-specific recommendations. He began with an expansive discussion of the types of parks that could be incorporated into a city plan, dividing them into six classes: first, the smallest parks, such as the triangles at street intersections; second, the ornamental squares that could take up part of a block and provide landscape beauty in the business district; third, the small playgrounds for young children, designed to include landscape beauty; fourth, playfields for older boys with ballfields and other facilities for active play; fifth, landscape parks big enough to provide a respite

LAKE UNION, SHOWING BALLARD AND FREMONT IN THE DISTANCE. SEATTLE.

View from Capitol Hill looking northwest across Lake Union toward Fremont and Ballard showing the development along the lakeshore as the city grew northward.

from city life; and sixth, large parks that preserved scenic beauty and excluded recognizably artificial elements as much as possible.

For Seattle, he recommended primarily developing parks of the fourth and fifth classes. He thought that these would provide the most benefit, and that undeveloped land beyond the city limits could provide access to the types of experiences within a reasonable distance that parks of the sixth class would offer. As he had mentioned in his 1903 report, "Seattle possesses extraordinary landscape advantages in having a great abundance and variety of water views and views of wooded hills and distant mountains and snow-capped peaks." These external features augmented even the smallest parks.

To decide on the locations and extent of parks and parkways in the annexed districts, Olmsted had to balance the need for parkland with each area's capacity to fund acquisitions. This was particularly true in Ballard, where he noted the residents' overall lower incomes. The park board decided they would not use any of the park bond money authorized prior to the annexations and funded by taxes on property within the city's original limits to purchase parkland in the newly annexed areas. At the same time, Olmsted determined that, prior to the recent annexations, the city had parkland that amounted to 3.25 percent of its total land mass. Although it was lower than the 5 percent average in American cities, he thought it would be reasonable to apply the same standard to the new neighborhoods, since it would bring parity with the older neighborhoods. He then used this standard

to identify acquisitions that would create a network of "local parks, especially for women with babies and for playgrounds for young children, within a short walk, say half a mile, of every home, and . . . playfields for boys of the grammar school age and outdoor gymnasiums for older boys within a mile of every home," and larger parks, particularly those on the saltwater shorelines of West Seattle and Ballard.

Olmsted began his recommendations with descriptions of the parkways extending from the drives outlined in the 1903 report. Just one section of new parkway in the north end would depart from the main boulevard just northwest of Woodland Park, traveling across the northern reaches of Ballard to Golden Gardens Park (then a private park at the end of a streetcar line). In the southeast part of the city, Lake Washington Boulevard would continue on as Brighton Beach Parkway to Dunlap Canyon, where Olmsted had it climb the hill to become the proposed South Ridge Boulevard, a "speedway" (or an expressway, somewhat like a highway) along the top of Beacon Hill. This drive would then drop down the hill to the west via Duwamish Hill Parkway to South Park, crossing over the river valley to West Seattle Parkway, which would pass over the hill to the West Seattle business district, where it would become Sound Bluffs Parkway and wind down the hill to what later became Schmitz Park and on to Alki Beach. From Jefferson Park on Beacon Hill, Olmsted's plan had the South Seattle Parkway cross the river valley and connect with the Duwamish Head Parkway, following the shoreline to Alki Point. He located a park in the Longfellow neighborhood (in the valley extending south from Youngstown), and on Puget Sound, called for a large park at Williams Point (first called West Seattle Park, now Lincoln Park) and another at Alki Point. In Magnolia, he outlined the boundaries of a Magnolia Bluffs Park that would have been much larger than today's Magnolia Park and included the bluffs above the beach and below the boulevard. In addition to these recommendations, Olmsted described a plan to phase the additional park system development as funding allowed to expand the extent of parkland along the parkways.

The report ended with a list of parks and playfields for the annexed areas: Ballard Bluff Park (Sunset Hill Park and adjacent portion of Sunset Hill Greenbelt), Isaac Parker Playfield (Ballard Playground), Market Street Playfield (Gilman Playground), Whitman Playfield (site in Crown Hill not acquired), Ravenna Park, Pigeon Point Park (site is small area at north tip of West Duwamish Greenbelt today), Duwamish Head Park (Hamilton Viewpoint Park), Alki Point Park (area includes Bar-S Playground and Alki Treatment Plant today), Forest Park (Schmitz Preserve Park), West Seattle Playfield (Hiawatha Playfield), South Park Playfield (site not acquired, but South Park Playground seven blocks north was), York Playfield (proposed site was two blocks south of current location), Headland Park (Stan Sayres Memorial Park and Genesee Park), Columbia Playfield (Rainier Playfield), Bailey Peninsula Park (Seward Park), Graham Avenue Playfield (site not acquired, but Brighton Playfield

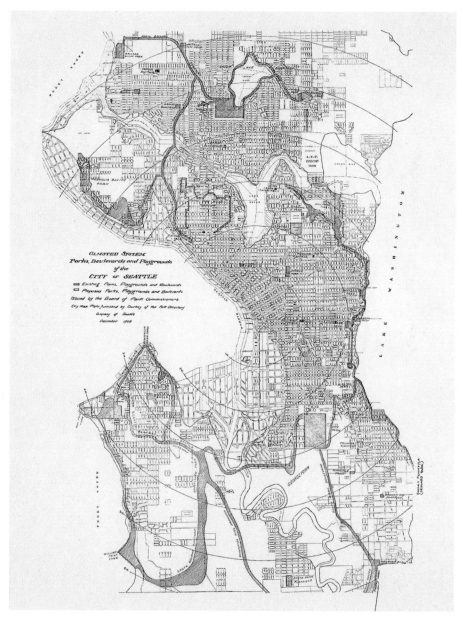

Map of Seattle showing the recommended expansion of the park and boulevard system outlined in Olmsted's 1908 supplemental report.

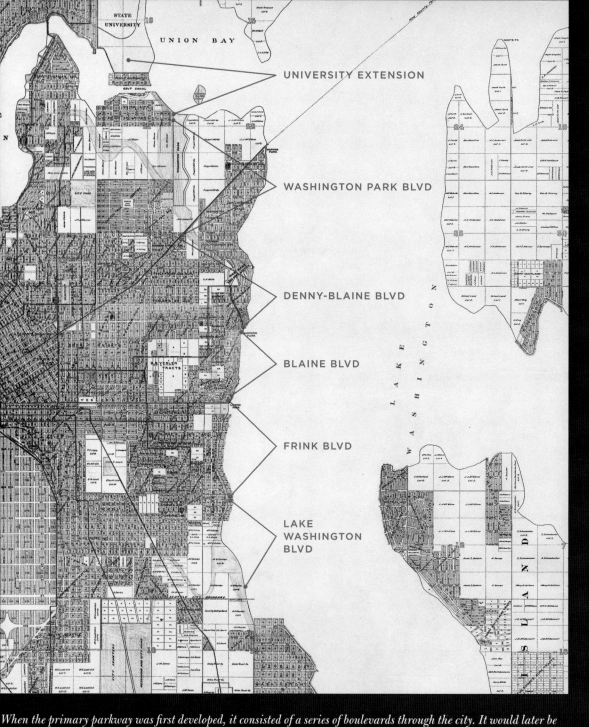

UNIVERSITY EXTENSION

WASHINGTON PARK BLVD

DENNY-BLAINE BLVD

BLAINE BLVD

FRINK BLVD

LAKE
WASHINGTON
BLVD

When the primary parkway was first developed, it consisted of a series of boulevards through the city. It would later be renamed Lake Washington Boulevard from Seward Park to Montlake Boulevard.

north of Graham Street was), Dunlap Canyon Playfield (site not acquired, but Rainier Beach Playfield is located to the east), City Park Addition to Atlantic City (Beer Sheva Park), Pritchard Island (Pritchard Island Beach and Rainier Beach Urban Farm and Wetlands), Rainier Shore Park (site not acquired, near Lakeridge Playfield), Rainier Playfield (site just north of Hutchinson Playground), South Ridge Playfield (Van Asselt Playfield at former school), Beacon Hill Playfield (Van Asselt Playground), Mount Baker Playfield (Franklin High School Playfield), and Southwest Playfield (near the now-demolished South Seattle School).

As Olmsted prepared his new report, development of the 1903 plan elements continued. The park board felt some urgency because they wanted to have as much of the parks and parkways system developed as possible before the opening of the Alaska-Yukon-Pacific Exposition in June 1909. In particular, the park board wanted to open the boulevard on Lake Washington's shoreline to provide a park drive to the fair grounds. To that end, the park board worked on the different sections of the parkway as right-of-way could be acquired. Each section had a different name, despite it being a continuous drive. From 43rd Avenue South, near today's Stan Sayres Memorial Park, to Colman Park it was known as Lake Washington Boulevard. Bypassing the residential development along Lakeside Avenue, the Frink Boulevard section left the shoreline at Colman Park and looped its way up the hill, through the park,

and then directly north across the slope to Frink Park. At the north end of Frink Park, near Yesler Way, the boulevard angled down the hill to the lake again just north of Leschi Park, then still a private park at the end of a streetcar line. From that point, the Blaine Boulevard section followed the lakeshore to just north of Madrona Park, where it became Denny-Blaine Boulevard until it reached Washington Park at East Madison Street. From there it became Washington Park Boulevard until, at the northwest corner of Washington Park, the University Extension (a portion of which would soon be renamed Montlake Boulevard) began, which then crossed via the Montlake isthmus to the south entrance of the Alaska-Yukon-Pacific Exposition, ending at a plaza where Pacific Street meets Montlake Boulevard today. Along its way, it touched upon or passed through Colman, Leschi, Frink, Mount Baker, Madrona, Viretta, Denny-Blaine, Lakeview, and Washington Parks.

The route of the University Extension through Montlake met with some resistance from the property owners there. Olmsted wanted the parkway to follow the shoreline from what is today the northeast corner of Washington Park to the north side of the planned Montlake Cut. That plan would be complicated when the Army Corps of Engineers' Seattle District Engineer Hiram Chittenden restricted any bridge crossing of the cut to an alignment with 22nd Avenue North (today's Montlake Boulevard NE alignment). In the end, the property owners at Montlake agreed to donate the land for a boulevard through the middle of the isthmus and for parks at each end of the residential neighborhood, which would become East Montlake Park and West Montlake Park.

In May 1908 the park commissioners decided to hire an assistant superintendent to construct and manage playgrounds. They promoted Frank L. Fuller, who had been the secretary to the board. They also hired J. Howard Stine as the Director of Playgrounds to manage the playground supervisors who were hired at the urging of women's clubs. The supervisors did more than just ensure children's safety. In fact, it could be argued that safety was secondary. When, in 1911, the park board received a letter from Dr. Park Weed Willis about a little boy injured by a swing and suggesting the dangerous equipment be removed, the park board secretary was directed "to reply . . . that there were a number of movable devises [sic] on the playground which would injure persons who might get in the way and that it would hardly be fair to remove those appliances because of the fact that a few persons might not use proper precautions." Instead, playground supervisors organized games and encouraged sportsmanship to instill moral values in the children. The 1907-1908 Park Department annual report extolled the increased use of facilities and reduced incidence of foul language at the playgrounds.

The park commissioners began that annual report with a description of their playground work because, "As the question of providing playfields both for the larger as well as the smaller children is occupying the attention of the country at large, and, as we are

endeavoring to meet the demand in Seattle, it may not be amiss to consider this phase of the year's work first." They explained the developments at the Lincoln Park (Cal Anderson), Hill Tract, Denny-Fuhrman (Rogers), Pendleton Miller, and B. F. Day playgrounds. Each had different facilities and equipment, determined by the primary users of each site, including tennis courts, swings, sand courts, "teeter boards," horseshoe pits, handball and basketball courts, and climbing equipment. They also reported irrigation, drainage, and grading improvements.

Work at Cowen Park and the viewpoint at the top of Frink Park, guided by Olmsted plans, was underway in 1908. The Panic of 1907 had a lingering effect on the local economy, and the Park Department put unemployed men to work in the parks, doing the hard labor of grubbing out understory plants, building paths, and cutting trees. In Volunteer Park, the annual report said, Thompson was implementing the Olmsted Brothers' planting plan, but as they had not prepared such a formal plan by that time, it is unclear what he was working from. It is likely that he talked with Dawson about the basic outlines of the park's design described in the 1904 preliminary plan and began work on that. The water tower had been built at the site Olmsted recommended and the mounded earth around it planted with shrubs and trees.

All told, quite a bit of work was completed with the influx of bond money and the regular park fund revenues by the end of 1908. Their efforts were bolstered by donations of land for Schmitz Park

Plat of the Montlake Park Addition, filed June 1908, showing the location of Montlake Boulevard, park drives, and parks in the new neighborhood. This arrangement of public spaces allowed the park system boulevard to cross the isthmus in alignment with the location authorized by the Army Corps of Engineers for the Lake Washington Ship Canal crossing while still reserving some of the shoreline for public use.

Montlake Boulevard Design Recommendations

As the city prepared for the Alaska-Yukon-Pacific Exposition, one of the key infrastructure projects was the construction of a streetcar line from downtown to the south entrance of the fair via the Montlake isthmus. Once the park board had made an agreement with the property owners that the park boulevard would cross the isthmus in the center of the planned subdivision, they turned to Olmsted for advice on the layout of the street. He sent a letter in January 1909 providing guidance on placement of the streetcar line and other boulevard elements. Because this section of the boulevard passed through a residential area, he suggested a more formal layout than he would for other portions of the parkway. He recommended placing the streetcar tracks in the middle of the center strip, "as has been done in Boston of late years," if the streetcar company would agree to place rails below the surface as much as possible so they would not be visible. He advised that "the trolley poles should be of steel of especial architectural design, firmly set in a perfectly vertical position" and placed "in two rows, lining up with rows of trees." From east to west, the profile of the boulevard should be: Two feet of turf, 9 feet of sidewalk, 14 feet of turf and trees, 24 feet of roadway, with trees planted to allow the street to be widened to 32 feet at a later date, a central parking street of 54 feet, another 14-foot-wide turf and tree strip, an 8-foot sidewalk, and two feet for a turf strip. He recommended tulip trees for all four rows of trees and that "moderate amounts of shrubbery, mainly of small growing sorts, and vines should be grown up the trolley poles and electric lighting poles." In addition to his recommendation for the right-of-way, he suggested restrictions for the adjacent residential lots: a 40-foot setback, single-family houses built no higher than three stories, and no liquor sales or commercial uses.

Montlake Boulevard originally had a wider median to accommodate streetcar tracks before it was narrowed to make room for additional vehicular lanes in the 1950s.

Playground at Salmon Bay Park in Ballard, 1910.

in West Seattle by park commissioner Ferdinand Schmitz and his wife, Emma, in January 1908, and a thousand feet of shoreline south of the Mount Baker neighborhood by Charles B. Dodge, for the extension of the lakeshore boulevard, in April. This created strong momentum for a $1 million bond measure on the December 1908 special election ballot. While it was twice the amount of the first bond measure, Austin E. Griffiths, president of the Seattle Playground Association, thought the park board should ask for several million dollars for boulevard, small park, and playground acquisition and development, telling Mayor John F. Miller in an open letter quoted in *The Seattle Times* that "comparatively few of the poorer children or their parents use the larger parks on the outskirts of the city, and . . . the playgrounds should be near the congregated centers." Griffiths' request was backed by the Salmon Bay, Ross, Youngstown, Brighton Beach, and South Park improvement clubs, all of which wanted local parks constructed.

The Seattle Star also supported the measure, arguing it was an "investment for the moral and physical welfare of generations to come." If the measure did not pass, they claimed, it would be because of voters' "failure to do one's duty to humanity." Voters, however, did their "duty to humanity" and the bond passed easily in the December 29, 1908, election. It received majorities in all 14 wards, with a tally of 6,688 votes in favor to 2,359 votes against.

John Olmsted returned to Seattle on December 30 of that year to tend to preparations for the world's fair and park system projects. While he was in Seattle, two big ideas bubbled up. The first, a central park in

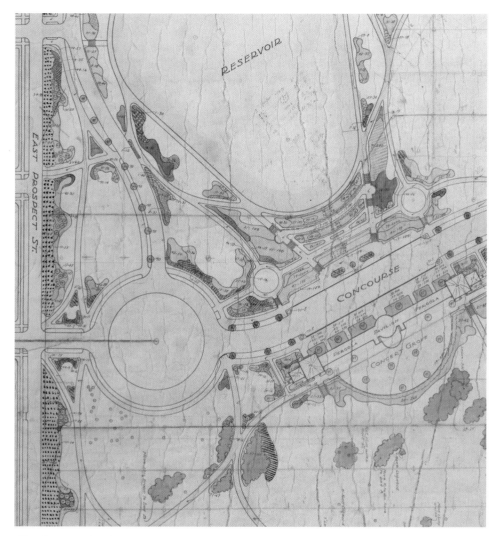

Children on teeter-totters in Hiawatha Playfield, 1912.

The planting plan for Volunteer Park, completed in 1910, shows the plants and trees designated for planting beds, along with the areas to be covered with turf to create greenswards. This detail from the plan shows the area along the concourse's southern end, including the mound on which the water tower would sit, the more formal flower beds around the lily pond and adjacent to the reservoir, and the trees that would form the allée along the drive.

the downtown core, received Olmsted's endorsement, but floundered due to the high costs associated with it. Civic leaders had identified a large tract of land on the slope between the King County Courthouse and City Hall, bounded by James Street and Yesler Way and 6th and 8th Avenues. Olmsted suggested reducing the size to make it more affordable, but that did not solve the funding difficulties.

The second idea brought together all the elements of the City Beautiful movement, including parks, iconic architecture, grand public spaces, and comprehensive transportation networks. On January 28, 1909, the Washington Chapter of the American Institute of Architects formed the Municipal Plans League to promote an idea that had been around since at least 1907, when Charles Bebb, of the prominent architecture firm Bebb & Mendel, invited Olmsted to attend a meeting with the Committee of the Representative Bodies of the Public Interests of Seattle about establishing a civic center in Seattle. Bebb chaired the 1909 meeting at which the vision for the league was further developed. Bebb was quoted in *The Seattle Times* as explaining that "with the conviction that the rapid extension of the city is bound to continue indefinitely, grave apprehension is aroused for its future welfare, unless, at an early date, its physical growth be brought under the guidance and control of sympathetic insight into its present condition and bold foresight for the future." In addition to the architects, Olmsted, attorney John W. Roberts, Professor Frederick M. Padelford of the University of Washington's English Department, engineer James D. Blackwell, attorney Charles E.

Remsberg, and others who attended the meeting "heartily endorsed" the plan.

The Municipal Plans League and its initiative mirrored national trends. Other American cities of all sizes were developing plans to bring order to the rapid urbanization and industrialization they were experiencing. Seattle, the league members believed, needed to draw on national experts, such as Olmsted and Daniel Burnham of Chicago, who had served as the Director of Works for the 1893 Columbian Exposition, considered to be the model for the City Beautiful movement, and who had brought those ideas to bear on the development of Chicago.

Seattle voters approved a charter amendment in March 1910 to form the Municipal Plans Commission. It was assumed that Olmsted would be one of several experts involved, but R. H. Thomson, in his role on the executive committee, pulled strings behind the scenes and brought on just one person to develop the city plan, civil engineer Virgil Bogue. Bogue brought years of experience designing port plans and engineering railroad grades and tunnels to the project. He was familiar with the Olmsted firms' work, and he referenced the Seattle park system plans in his report and extended the planned parkways beyond the city limits. When Bogue's report, the *Plan of Seattle*, came to a public vote in 1912, it would be soundly defeated due to a number of factors, not the least of which was the all-or-none nature of the vote, which contrasted starkly with how the Olmsted plans were presented and adopted.

With the influx of funding from the park bonds in early 1909, the park board pushed forward

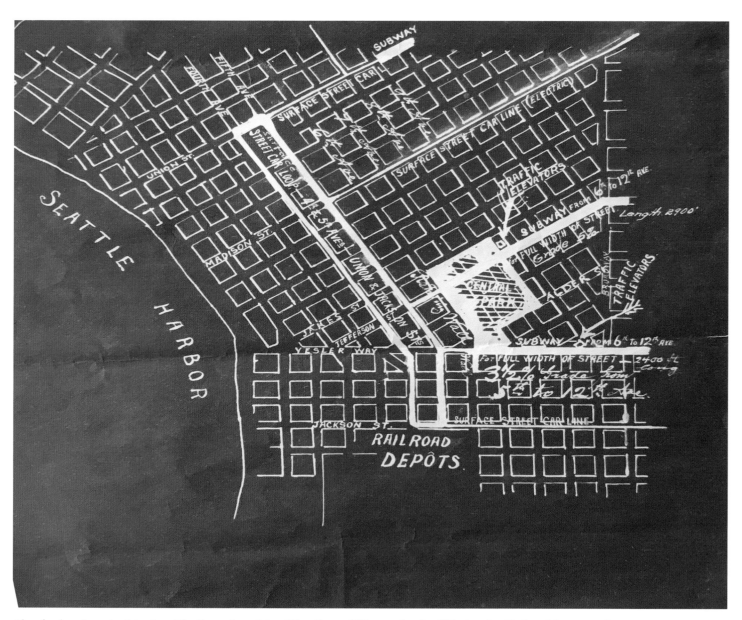

Plan for downtown park proposed for the western slope of Courthouse Hill, now the site of Harborview Park and Interstate 5.

Map from the Plan of Seattle *showing Existing and Proposed Park and Park Boulevards and Proposed Rapid Transit Routes, including the Olmsted parkways and boulevards and the extension of them beyond the city limits, 1911.*

development and readied the system for world's fair visitors, who, it was hoped, would be so impressed with the natural beauty and bounty of Seattle and Washington state that they would decide to move to the region. In the Park Department's annual report for 1909, the list of improved parks had grown impressively and included: Woodland, Washington, Volunteer, Schmitz, Kinnear, Mount Baker, Frink, Denny, Leschi and Madrona (both added to the system by purchase), Interlaken, Denny-Blaine, Salmon Bay, and Atlantic (Beer Sheva) Parks.

In February 1909, the park board approved the route of Jefferson Boulevard (later renamed Cheasty Boulevard), connecting Jefferson Park to Mount Baker Boulevard (which would be extended from 30th Avenue to Rainier Avenue in 1910). In many ways, this linked series of boulevards, from Beacon Avenue (which bisects Jefferson Park) to Lake Washington Boulevard, is the embodiment of Olmstedian ideals. It travels from a park with expansive views of downtown, Elliott Bay, and the Olympic Mountains in the distance, through a forested hillside (Cheasty Boulevard) to a residential neighborhood that largely exemplifies Olmsted's vision for the melding of residential and park land (Mount Baker Boulevard), down through another park to Lake Washington Boulevard, with its views across the water to the Cascade Mountains. It captures the "genius of place" that is unique to Seattle's location and topography.

The 1909 annual report list of parks that had been acquired, but not yet developed, showed the rapid expansion of the system. In the central part of the city, land had been donated by the Colman Estate,

Rustic bridge across a ravine in Schmitz Park near Alki Beach, 1910.

extending the parkland up the hill from the pumping station on the lakeshore to form Colman Park. A number of parks, including Columbia, Dearborn, Evergreen (David Rodgers), Green Lake, Ballard Bluff (Sunset Hill), Greenwood (likely a park that was at the site of today's Phinney Neighborhood Association), Montlake, Roanoke, Pigeon Point (at the tip of the West Duwamish Greenbelt), Sturgus, Yesler (possibly the park located at that time at 13th Avenue and East Yesler Way or at the site of Pratt Park today), and Phelps (no longer extant, but located near today's Marshall Park), expanded the park system in the city's neighborhoods.

The park board differentiated between the playfields and playgrounds, although today they are more often described as playfields and parks. The former were larger and had facilities for older kids, often ballfields. The latter were smaller and had

South Park Playfield and fieldhouse, 1910.

lawns and play areas suitable for younger children. The park board planned to build playfields in the Columbia City, South Park, University District, Alki, Rainier Beach, Central District, and Queen Anne neighborhoods. The South Seattle, Youngstown (Delridge), Interbay, Brighton Beach, and Walla Walla (Garfield) playgrounds were also planned. In West Seattle, the park commissioners were in negotiations for the Tull Tract, a two-block area near the West Seattle business district that would become Hiawatha Playfield.

When Olmsted returned in June 1909 for the opening of the Alaska-Yukon-Pacific Exposition, the park commissioners asked him to review the work done on the Interlaken, Washington Park, Montlake, and Lake Washington drives. Olmsted wrote a report that was largely critical of the engineers' work (primarily George Cotterill and Park Department engineer Samuel Lancaster developed the alignment and landscaping plans). He thought the corners were too sharp, the lines "conspicuously stiff and formal," and structures like retaining walls and bridges too refined. For pedestrians, he wrote,

> *there has been what seems to me a most undesirable omission of a walk paralleling nearly all of these drives. My experience in parks elsewhere leaves me without the slightest doubt that it is essential for the pleasure and convenience both of drivers and of pedestrians that such a walk should be provided everywhere along these drives, with the possible exception of some portion of the drive in the water works property [Colman Park], where the curves are so numerous that there is little likelihood that pedestrians would be tempted to follow them continuously, but would be willing to cut across from one loop to another by means of flights of steps, supplemented by steep walks for baby carriages and those who do not wish to use the steps.*

He reminded the park board that the character of the drives in parks should be as natural as possible, with trees planted irregularly and native plants covering the slopes.

The newspaper reporter covering the park board meeting where Olmsted's letter was discussed tried to smooth over its harsh tone by explaining, "Olmsted is said to leave praise to others and to confine himself to pointing out defects. Almost all his points were acknowledged to be well taken by the board." But the criticisms exposed a challenge the park board faced in realizing the Olmsted vision for the park system. Where they could hire the Olmsted Brothers firm to prepare preliminary plans or ask for direction from Dawson, they had site-specific guidance to follow. For those parks like Volunteer and Frink where they also commissioned planting and grading plans, and even some architectural drawings, little was left to interpretation and a cohesive landscape developed. Where they had only recommendations from the 1903 or 1908 reports, the commissioners had to rely on Thompson and Lancaster, and sometimes Cotterill, none of them landscape architects, to apply Olmsted principles. The additional challenges posed by rising land prices also limited the full implementation of Olmsted's vision. Boulevards had less room to meander, rights-of-way were reduced and parks' extents limited. For example, the parkway between Madison Street and Denny-Blaine had to be narrowed and the sweeping switchbacks down the hill had to be tightened. It is beautiful in its own way, but it lacks the expansiveness that Olmsted intended.

Recently completed Interlaken Boulevard, 1909.

This 1910 photograph shows the turn from West Galer Street to Thorndyke Avenue, which served as the link between Interbay and Magnolia in Olmsted's primary park boulevard that connected Fort Lawton (later Discovery Park) and Bailey Peninsula (later Seward Park).

Although Olmsted had given recommendations for the Magnolia Bluffs boulevard in his 1903 and 1908 reports, opposition by James Clise, who owned a large portion of the bluffs and adjacent tidelands, prevented its development according to Olmsted's vision. In April 1909, the park board adopted an altered route laid out by Lancaster. This alignment followed Olmsted's up the east side of Magnolia via Thorndyke Avenue to a viewpoint park overlooking Smith Cove and continued around to the Wolf Creek ravine. There, instead of heading down the face of the bluff, the parkway route stayed on top, following its edge in and out of the ravines that jutted into the hillside, before turning inland toward Fort Lawton. This routing resolved the conflict with Clise but abandoned any hope of having the parkland

After the Alaska-Yukon-Pacific Exposition, the university made use of a number of buildings, including the Forestry Building (top photo taken from its roof, looking to the southwest), which became the new home of the Washington State Museum, and the Music Pavilion (bottom), shown here just to the left of Rainier Vista, a landscape design feature of the fair that continues to shape the character of the campus today.

encompass the bluffs, beach, and tidelands out to West Point. The acquisition stalled as negotiations continued until 1911, when Clise offered to donate the land for the boulevard if the city agreed not to condemn the bluffs, beach, or tidelands. Olmsted did not think this was a good idea because he preferred that the boulevard run partway down the bluffs for a portion of its route around Magnolia, but the city acquiesced.

After the burst of work preparing for the world's fair visitors, spending the park bonds, and developing playgrounds and playfields, the park board did not rest. In October 1909 the commissioners and the Board of Regents for the University of Washington reached an agreement to lease the fair's grounds, primarily the lower portion of the campus, to the Park Department for use as a public park. The university would continue to use the upper campus, the permanent buildings from the fair, and some of the temporary ones, as classroom and office space. The planting beds from the fair suffered somewhat from pilfering, but the groves of trees, the lawns, and the paths remained intact and provided an expanse of parkland on the hillside and the lakeshores for the public to enjoy.

At the end of the year, the park board considered increasing their planned $2 million bond measure to $2.5 million in order to fund the acquisitions and development of the central park proposed for Courthouse Hill. Park commissioners Edward Cheasty and Ambrose Ernst opposed this idea, possibly because it might make it less likely that the already-large bond would be approved by voters. The

$2 million bond was approved with a margin of nearly two to one at the special election on March 8, 1910.

Although the park board reported difficulty selling the park bonds, the park system continued to grow in 1910. In March, Cheasty shared correspondence he had received from Washington Senator Samuel Piles and Secretary of War Jacob M. Dickinson about the possibility of public use of Fort Lawton. It was common for the public to visit the parade ground at the fort and the beach and lighthouse at West Point, and the park commissioners wanted to extend the Magnolia Bluffs parkway through the fort. The Army agreed to have Olmsted develop a plan for the fort, which he delivered in July 1910. The plan shows bluff and woodland drives snaking through the military base and some recreational facilities at the West Point beach and some other adjustments to the fort's arrangement, but it was filed away and not implemented.

In April 1910, the Washington State Art Association came to the park board and asked to place a Museum of Arts and Sciences in Volunteer Park, either in the lawn north of the reservoir or at the north end of the concourse, between the Seward statue and the cemetery. The conservatory had not yet been built, so there was an open space at the end of the concourse drive. The museum would require a 200-by-220-foot space from the city. The park commissioners referred the question to the Municipal Plans Commission, which was planning a civic center in the Denny Regrade area as part of the effort to develop the *Plan of Seattle* (commonly referred to as the Bogue Plan). In October, the commission and

Olmsted determined it would be better to put such a building with other similar facilities in the civic center near Lake Union. Olmsted wrote to board president John T. Heffernan that, while his sympathies lay with the museum's intentions, he could not approve the placement of a museum, particularly one so large, in a landscape park because it would be too injurious to the character of the park and visitors' experiences.

In May 1910, the park board asked Olmsted to prepare a report on playground development in the city. The park board had invested in a number of playgrounds and playfields, but the neighborhood improvement clubs continued to clamor for more, particularly in the recently annexed areas. He submitted his report in October 1910, again in the form of a letter to the Board of Park Commissioners. He briefly discussed the playground movement in American cities, and wrote, "It is true that the City needs and must have playgrounds. It may be an exaggeration to say that they are a matter of life and death but they surely are necessary as a matter of public health and good morals." But, he continued, it was important to make a distinction between playgrounds as public parks and schoolyards, warning, "If the Park Board diverts its income from park work to teaching children in playgrounds, it is not accomplishing what it should in its proper line and is doing what should properly be done and what could probably be better done by the School Board."

Further, he stated that playground development should include only those elements such as baseball fields, lawns for croquet or tennis, sand courts, "or similar things harmonious with or not

Hiawatha Playfield

Originally named West Seattle Playfield when it was first developed in 1910, Hiawatha Playfield was organized into distinct areas. The ballfield, which filled the center of the park, provided space for organized team sports, such as baseball. The outdoor gymnasium, along the eastern border of the park and segregated by gender, offered equipment and space for individual activities, including a wading pool "for large children." It lay adjacent to the fieldhouse, which had an indoor gymnasium, a performance space, and rooms for clubs and classes. The playground in the northeast corner catered to smaller children, with a wading pool, smaller apparatus, and benches for caretakers. A double tennis court lay at the northern center of the park. The rest of the perimeter of the park was given over to paths, lawns, and trees, with planting beds along the borders. The playfield's northern edge was filled with trees with a parklike atmosphere.

The playfield has evolved over time. The running track was relocated in the 1930s. The lawn east of the fieldhouse was used for housing troops during World War II, likely leading to the removal of the outdoor gymnasium apparatus. The fieldhouse was enlarged in 1949. The ballfield was enlarged and resurfaced with artificial turf and a new running track in 2009. Despite these changes, the original Olmsted intent—a space for organized sports balanced with passive recreation—has been maintained. The playfield was designated a city landmark in 1984.

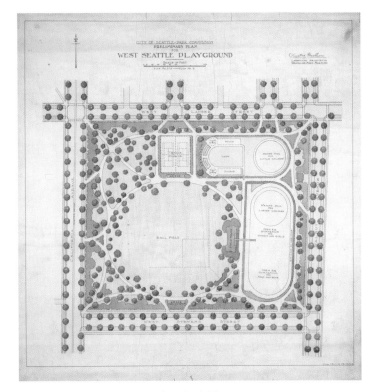

Preliminary plan for Hiawatha Playfield, 1910.

Hiawatha Playfield featured facilities for athletic games and other types of organized play, but also had landscaped areas that provided respite from the city's noise and congestion.

unduly injurious to the landscape of the park." The playground parks, he believed, should be large enough to include meandering paths, groves of trees, planting beds, and other park elements. Hiawatha Park, in West Seattle, was the first full-fledged playfield developed with a fieldhouse in Seattle. Several more would soon follow, starting with the Ballard, South Park, and Collins playfields. All of the playfields incorporated park elements along with athletic facilities.

In the fall of 1910, years of efforts to acquire Bailey Peninsula in the south and Ravenna Park in the north finally culminated in successful condemnation proceedings. Owners of the tracts, both featuring significant stands of timber in a largely cutover city, asked what the park board felt were exorbitant prices in contentious negotiations that stretched out with offers and counteroffers. The issue had been further complicated in the spring of 1909 when city council member Eugene W. Way, chair of the park and boulevard committee, refused to consider any ordinances authorizing the Ravenna Park condemnation until acquisition of Bailey Peninsula was underway. He echoed some residents' concerns that the northern part of the city, with its parkways, the world's fair grounds, Woodland Park, and Washington Park, was getting a disproportionate share of park investments.

Throughout the system, the park board continued implementing the 1903 and 1908 plans with a variety of projects. Efforts to build a connection between Montlake and Ravenna Boulevards came to a head in August and September 1911 after years of discussions about extending the park boulevard

A concrete ring surrounds the mineral springs located alongside the creek in Ravenna Park in about 1910. The ring is still visible at a junction of trails in the park, but the springs no longer flow at that location.

through campus. One effort, spearheaded at the state level, sought to run the parkway parallel to the Northern Pacific tracks on the east side of campus. Montlake Boulevard would then connect to Ravenna Boulevard via a new street, Ravenna Place. The legislature granted a right-of-way for the drive to the city, and Thompson wrote to Olmsted that "this scheme is already established and will undoubtedly be carried out." But Thompson conveyed the hope of the park board that "you are able to work out an alternative route directly across the University Grounds from Montlake to 17th Avenue NE (University Boulevard) in such a way as will be satisfactory to the Regents." Olmsted replied that he was working on a revised campus plan, but the temporary fair buildings retained for continued use had complicated his plan to carry the parkway across the northern portion of the campus. He laid out its route across the northeastern corner to NE 45th Street just east of 20th Avenue NE. This corresponds

Ravenna Park
When Olmsted first visited Seattle, the privately owned Ravenna Park was outside the city limits. Its location between the University of Washington and Green Lake made it a natural candidate for inclusion in the park system, however. In the 1903 report Olmsted praised the park: "The tract known as Ravenna Park is mainly composed of a deep ravine, and is wholly covered with native forest, which is remarkable in that there has been much less destruction of the large trees by woodchoppers, and of the undergrowth and trees by fires than at any other equally accessible point in or about the city." Within the relatively untouched forest, Ravenna Park boasted several enormous Douglas firs. The park's owners, William and Louise Beck, named the trees and promoted the park with brochures featuring the behemoths. One tree—274 feet tall and 44 feet in circumference—was named "Roosevelt Tree" in honor of President Theodore Roosevelt. Others were named Paderewski, Robert E. Lee (400 feet tall), Adam, McDowell, Pan, and the Siamese Twins. Two close-growing trees were named for the city's vice-tolerating mayor Hiram Gill and vice-abhorring Reverend Mark Matthews.

While the park was not designed by Olmsted, it plays a key role in the park system. The boulevard runs along its southern end and then meets up with the adjoining Cowen Park at its western end. It also, in a very Olmstedian way, provides a wooded retreat enhanced by the sights and sounds of ponded and flowing water.

Seward Park

One of the last park designs Olmsted developed for Seattle was for Seward Park. Completed in 1912, it incorporated elements that took advantage of the forested interior and the lakeshore that encircled the peninsula. Beginning at the entrance, which was still seasonally blocked by a narrow waterway, making the peninsula an island before the lowering of the lake following the opening of the Montlake Cut in 1916, a small bridge carried visitors into the park. To its south, about where the tennis courts are today, Olmsted located three docks—one for motorboats, one for ferries, and one for commercial use. A loop drive followed the shoreline around the finger of land, providing access to boat landings, harbors, beaches, summer houses, and the views across the lake. Drives through the "Magnificent Forest" provided access to an observation tower and a woodland pond. Pathways meandered through the forest and down to the shoreline from the loop drive. At the north end, near the small-boat and motorboat harbors, a recreation area offered a basketball court, playground equipment, bathhouses for men and women, and a dancing pavilion.

Although a loop drive, the interior paths, and the allocation of space to different activities in the Olmsted plan would be realized in the park, the structural facilities were largely left on the drawing board. In later years, the Audubon Society would establish a nature education center in the former concession stand called the Seward Park Inn, built in 1927. A fish hatchery was built in the 1930s and operated until 1997. A bathhouse built in 1927 and expanded in 1940 became an arts studio in the 1970s. The amphitheater was added in 1953. A small playground built near the entrance was expanded in the 2000s. The biggest difference between the park Olmsted envisioned and the park today is the proliferation of parking lots, built to accommodate the rising popularity of automobiles in the years since Olmsted designed the site.

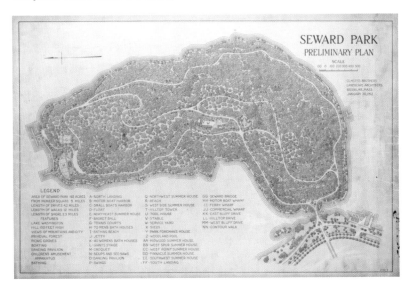

Preliminary plan for Seward Park, 1912.

in part to Mason Road and Whatcom Lane on campus today. The extension of Seward Avenue from the Exposition plan would provide a separate, less formal, internal drive on the campus to connect with Moore's University Boulevard (17th Avenue Northeast).

A joint committee of faculty and regents reviewed the plan and identified aspects of the Olmsted Brothers' preliminary plan recommendations that should be adopted, including having the library as a central architectural feature and adopting the Collegiate Gothic architectural style for campus buildings. After this review, however, the university hired architectural firm Bebb & Gould to develop a new revised plan. Carl Gould, who established the university's Department of Architecture in 1914 and had been part of the review team for the Olmsted plan, took the lead on the project, submitting the new plan that same year. This shift was at least in part due to the challenging logistics of working with an out-of-town firm. A 1915 letter from university president Henry Suzzallo's secretary, E. B. Stevens, sent regrets that "Mr. Dawson was not able to stay with us sufficiently long to get full force of different suggestions which were made by the members of our faculty."

The Bebb & Gould plan formalized the layout and shifted the axial intersection point slightly to the south. It also showed an extension of University Boulevard into campus, which is now called Memorial Way. Stevens Way was extended north to 21st Avenue NE. It would later be brought across the north end of campus to Memorial Way. On the east side of campus, Montlake Boulevard ran east of the railroad tracks to a point near today's Pend Oreille Place NE where a roadway is shown continuing north to connect with Ravenna

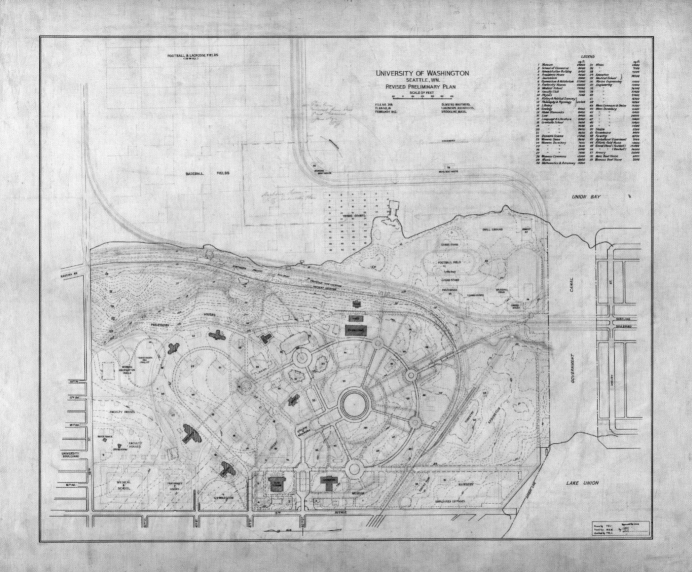

A preliminary plan study for a new University of Washington campus plan under development by John Olmsted in 1912. It shows the contour lines in orange and the existing buildings with diagonal-line fill and existing circulation routes in dashed and solid lines, with proposed buildings, drives, and walks in pencil. The final revised preliminary plan has not been found in the Olmsted Brothers' files, nor in the university's records.

Avenue NE. It is not clear if this connection was ever built, which would have provided for a more seamless park boulevard experience, with Montlake Boulevard serving as a link between Lake Washington Boulevard and Ravenna Boulevard. Sanborn insurance maps from the 1910s show it as a completed street, but there is no direct connection today.

Boulevard connections in the southern and southwestern parts of the city also proved challenging. As those neighborhoods developed, the park board began to look at how to carry the boulevard over the hills and connect the southern portions of the city. At the Alki Point end, Dawson met with Ferdinand Schmitz, the park commissioner who had donated parkland, to explain how the parkway could traverse the hill via a switchback leaving from Schmitz Park's northeast corner, if the park board could acquire more parkland to allow space for reasonable grades on the drive.

In the Delridge area, the Puget Mill Company owned a large tract of cutover land and they offered to donate some of it for a park and a parkway from the Duwamish River to 35th Avenue SW. The board hesitated to accept the donation because it was conditional on the city developing the parkway and park within five years, and presumably, if the Puget Mill Company determined they had not met that expectation, it could rescind the donation. This arrangement did not square with the legal requirement that the park board hold ownership of any land it developed because any investment of public money could be lost if the donation was nullified. The final resolution of the issue was not recorded in the Board of

Park Commissioners meeting minutes, but Puget Park and short sections of Puget Boulevard were formed out of the donated land. A lengthy section of the right-of-way for Puget Boulevard crossed through a parcel the mill company later sold to the city (today's Camp Long and the West Seattle Golf Course).

The parkway connection across the Duwamish River valley was not developed. No mention is made in Board of Park Commissioners minutes or Park Department planning records of a decision not to build the valley sections of either of the two proposed parkways, but it is telling that no alignments for parkways are included in the Duwamish River valley maps in the 1911 Bogue Plan. Instead, Map No. 7, of the Harbor Island and Duwamish River Districts, shows railroads, the channelization of the river, and other developments tailored to industrial uses.

Based on other discussions recorded in the board's meeting minutes, it seems that no improvement clubs or residents were asking for the parkways to be constructed, and they likely fell lower on the list of priorities. In time, the river valley would become heavily industrialized, making it even less likely that park boulevards would be developed between Beacon Hill and West Seattle. Harbor Avenue SW, now a scenic drive around Duwamish Head, fulfills Olmsted's intention for the park boulevard running along the shore to Alki Beach, but that vision would only be realized in the 1980s as commercial properties along the drive on the Elliott Bay shoreline were converted to parks.

At the end of 1911, the park board decided to ask for an additional $500,000 in park bonds, and voters approved the measure on March 5, 1912. A park board resolution listed the parks and parkways they planned to fund with the remaining $500,000 from the previous bond measure combined with the new funding. The list included condemnation payments for the lakeshore boulevard from the Mount Baker neighborhood to Seward Park, the shoreland around Bailey Peninsula, the right-of-way for Jefferson (Cheasty) Boulevard, the Youngstown (Delridge) and Hillman City (Brighton) playfields, and additional land for Hiawatha Playfield and for Denny-Blaine Park on Lake Washington. Planned acquisitions included playfield sites for South Seattle and Interbay, and payments for Jefferson Park, Mercer Playfield, Yesler Triangle (Prefontaine Place), and Leschi and Madrona Parks. Finally, they listed planned improvements to 19 parks, parkways, and playgrounds.

A year later, the Park Department's annual report reflects a Seattle park system that was filling out and fulfilling the recommendations of the system plans and the 1910 playground report. A total of 28 parks, 24 miles of improved boulevards, 22 playgrounds, 4 fieldhouses, and the Alki Bathing Beach had been developed. As *The Seattle Times* would crow in 1913, "Seattle's boulevard system is the talk of the country . . . and that the scenic settings have been provided for in every particular is indicated by the enthusiasm with which every visitor speaks of the park and boulevard system."

The following spring, the final piece of Lake Washington Boulevard fell into place. With some lobbying in Olympia, the park board and George Cotterill, by then Seattle's mayor, were able to get the

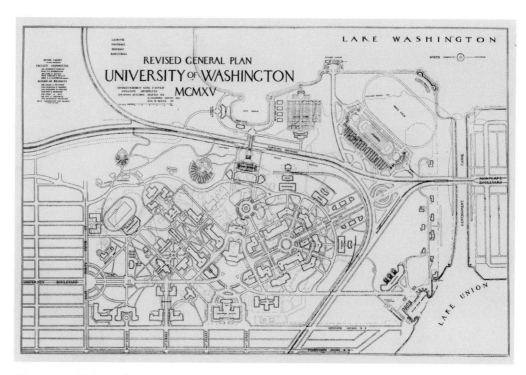

The 1915 Bebb & Gould Revised General Plan for the University of Washington campus, also known as the Regents Plan, drew significantly on the Olmsted Brothers' plan. It also introduced the extension of University Boulevard into the campus (today this drive is known as Memorial Way) and shifted the axial intersection slightly south, to today's Red Square.

shoreline between the Mount Baker neighborhood and Rainier Beach dedicated to the city. Olmsted and the park board tried to persuade the Rainier Beach Improvement Club and residents along the lake to support a shoreline alignment for the parkway south of Seward Park, but the business owners and residents wanted the drive to run on the uplands to Rainier Beach. Cotterill was successful, however, in getting the King County Board of Commissioners to agree to set aside the right-of-way for a parkway circling the entire lake, which was completed in 1922, although

Lake Washington Boulevard with trees planted along the lakeshore side, 1927.

parts of the right-of-way have been lost or altered by subsequent development.

By late 1913, the park board appeared to be slowing their expenditures. The financial tightening may explain a tense exchange of letters between the park board and the Olmsted Brothers firm. Roland Cotterill, secretary to the park board, wrote to the firm in April in response to a recently submitted bill for work done on Seattle's parks. He explained:

> *You have probably observed by our report that our extension funds are practically exhausted and that this year our expenditures for the first time in many years are confined to a budget which is being adhered to very closely. Through an oversight Mr. Thompson had failed to include in this budget an item covering the expense of your services and the Board seemed surprised at the amount of the bill [$5,749.72]. It was the concensus [sic] of opinion of the Board that inasmuch as our extension work was practically at an end that it would not be warranted in having any further improvement plans made for improvement work which may not be undertaken for years. Hence the notice to you to discontinue all work under way.*

The firm replied with a list of work that remained on the contracts for Green Lake Boulevard and Woodland, Schmitz, Seward, and Jefferson Parks. The park board did not reply with authorization for any further work, and the plan index cards in the archives at Fairsted (the former office of the Olmsted Brothers firm and the Olmsted family home in Brookline, Massachusetts) indicate that no plans were developed for any of these parks after 1912, although the firm continued working intermittently with the Board of Park Commissioners and helping shape the park and boulevard system for nearly three decades.

Olmsted in the Northwest

After Olmsted began working in the Pacific Northwest in 1903, he soon drew the attention of park commissioners, private homeowners, developers, and officials in charge of institutions across the region. After Portland and Seattle, Olmsted prepared a plan for Spokane's park system in 1908, although it would be held under wraps to limit land speculation until 1913. Taking advantage of the scenic Spokane River and Latah Creek, he laid out parkways and parks, gave advice on the city's 10 existing parks, and recommended 20 more. He developed plans for Adams (today's Cannon Hill), Liberty, and Corbin Parks. Liberty Park was later bisected by Interstate 90, but the other two are still excellent examples of Olmsted's vision for the city's parks. As in Seattle and Portland, Olmsted helped Spokane hire a park superintendent, John W. Duncan, from Boston, who would work on the city park system until his retirement in 1942.

Other projects for municipal and institutional clients included the University of Idaho, Whitman College, and Oregon State University campus plans, the Walla Walla park system, and Northern State Hospital in Sedro-Woolley. He would also cross the international border to complete a campus plan for the University of British Columbia and a design for Victoria Park. A full listing of

public projects in the Northwest can be found at OlmstedOnline.org.

Private clients, many of their projects managed by Fred Dawson, spanned the gamut from subdivisions to estates to residential lots. On Vancouver Island, he laid out the Uplands neighborhood with sweeping curved streets that followed the contours of the hills and provided views out to Mount Baker. In Seattle, he laid out the Uplands subdivision near Seward Park in 1924, and the Seattle Golf Club course and the adjacent community, The Highlands, in 1907, returning in 1929, when 40 acres were added to the subdivision. His projects extended to Portland, Tacoma, Bainbridge Island, and Idaho's Hayden Lake.

One of the private residences, the Dunn Gardens, is open to the public (on a limited basis). The 1915 Olmsted Brothers plan for the Dunn family's summer home, like a public landscape, incorporates a water feature, a variety of uses, views to Puget Sound, and layered plantings that include native species. Further, Olmsted coordinated the plan with the adjacent Agen family estate, which he had also designed, so the two landscapes would complement each other.

Extensive information about the private projects can be found in Catherine Joy Johnson's report "Olmsted in the Pacific Northwest."

The Dunn Gardens, a public garden in North Seattle, designed by Olmsted for the Dunn family estate in 1915.

The Uplands neighborhood in Victoria, British Columbia, designed by Olmsted in 1908.

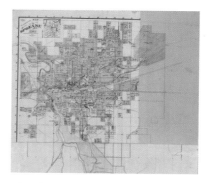

Plan for Spokane Parks outlined by John Olmsted in 1908 showing existing parks in orange shading and proposed parks and parkways in green shading.

Oregon State campus in Corvallis, Oregon, design developed by Olmsted Brothers in 1909.

Bridge along Lake Washington Boulevard in Frink Park.

CHAPTER 6
THE PARK SYSTEM AND THE MODERN CITY

Olmsted made his last visit to Seattle in 1911, but he continued to advise the park board through correspondence, and his associates made a number of trips to the city over the next several years. He provided advice on street trees that could be planted in honor of Seattleites who lost their lives in World War I and on the school district jurisdiction over playgrounds (he was opposed). His involvement declined significantly after the University of Washington Board of Regents shifted the campus planning project to Bebb & Gould. As the relationship between John Olmsted and the Board of Park Commissioners shifted, the park system shifted from a vision being realized into a defining element of the city's character and development.

Rick Olmsted made a trip to Seattle in November 1918 and consulted on improvements to McGraw Square, at the intersection of 5th Avenue and Westlake. The park commissioners who corresponded with him recognized his famous name and knew of his accomplishments, but do not appear to have developed any sort of ongoing relationship with him. Fred Dawson, however, knew a number of Seattleites and Superintendent Thompson well and served as the firm's primary liaison with the Board of Park Commissioners for many years. He wrote a number of letters regarding different projects and visited several times in the late 1910s and 1920s. He consulted on the advisability of acquiring Williams Point (Lincoln Park) in West Seattle in 1922, and corresponded with board chairman Albert S. Kerry in the late 1920s when the park board was considering hiring the firm again for a new park system plan.

Even though there would be this lingering involvement, 1914 marked a turning point for the park system and the Olmsted Brothers firm's relationship

Originally designed as a boulevard, the pedestrian and bicycle path added in the 1930s helped establish Green Lake as a beloved city park.

Lincoln Park, shown in this aerial view from 1965, provided access to the Puget Sound shoreline and reserved 106 acres of uplands for a local park, and, as Olmsted had anticipated in his 1908 report, "a recreation ground for the city as a whole."

commissioner George B. Lamping, announced that he would be reporting on changes that could be made to operations and that "new members of the board are of the opinion that there can be a large saving of money."

The park board would also have its first serious conflict with Superintendent Thompson in January 1914. The board called on Thompson to explain why trees had been cut down in Ravenna Park, including one of Ravenna's named trees, the Roosevelt. The park board meeting minutes indicate that the issue was settled by Thompson promising not to remove any further trees without approval from the park board, but the conflict may not have been fully resolved. In 1920, the park board accused him of insubordination and incompetence and asked for his resignation. Thompson chose to fight the firing under Civil Service Commission rules. While the dispute played out, former park commissioner Charles Saunders and Fred Dawson strategized in a series of letters about how they might help Thompson keep his job. Saunders met with editors—identified as "Col. Blethen," who had died in 1915, so likely one of his sons, C. B. or Joe, from *The Seattle Times* and James A. Wood from the *Seattle Post-Intelligencer*— and found each of them sympathetic to Thompson's situation but unable to campaign on his behalf in their editorial pages because of the mayor's political connection to *The Seattle Times* and anti-Thompson park commissioner James D. Lowman's business connection to the *Seattle Post-Intelligencer*. In early 1921 the Civil Service Commission ruled that Thompson had been fired for cause, and the park board appointed Jacob Umlauff, a park gardener, as interim superintendent.

with the park board. Longtime commissioners Edward Cheasty and John Frink died in June and September, respectively, and for the first time the park board had no members who had corresponded or worked closely with Olmsted. Commissioner Frank P. Mullen, the former city council member who had publicly opposed the park board's 1905 request for its first bond measure, proposed abandoning the Olmsted plan in December 1914. At the same park board meeting, the budget committee chair,

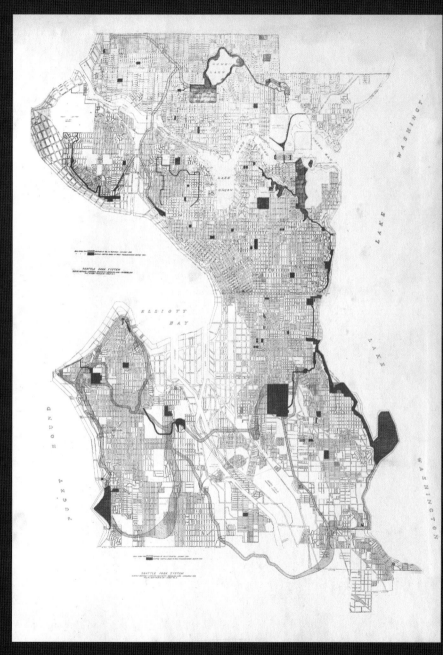

Map of Seattle showing the existing park system as of 1922 in blue shading and the parks and parkways proposed by Olmsted, but not yet developed, in blue cross-hatch lines. It was created in 1928 by Fred Dawson when he was in communication with A. S. Kerry, then president of the park board, about the possibility of the Olmsted Brothers developing a new park system plan for Seattle.

Baseball game at field in upper Woodland Park, 1913.

Eagle cage at Woodland Park Zoo, 1911.

The park board believed the superintendent role would best be filled by an engineer, dismissing the need for someone with a landscape architecture background. Dawson wrote to Charles Saunders that "to pick out a superintendent for the management and future development of the Seattle parks from a number of men all of whom are engineers and are recommended by the Seattle Chapter of the American Society of Engineers is little less than criminal." He wrote a shorter version of the same letter to Wood at the *Seattle Post-Intelligencer*, reiterating his concerns and sending him a letter that John Olmsted had written in 1909 about the issue. He implored Wood to bring the situation to the attention of the public. There is no evidence that Dawson swayed the park board, and over the next seven years, the department would have five different superintendents. None survived long in the position nor proved effective in doing more than maintaining the status quo in the park system.

While the Thompson conflict played out, the park board continued its work on the park system. They asked Dawson to inspect the park system and provide a report when he came to Seattle in 1917. Over a couple of days in late October he visited Woodland, Green Lake, Jefferson, and Seward Parks with Thompson and park board president Otto Roseleaf. At Woodland Park he suggested that the entrance gates already designed by the Olmsted Brothers be built, possibly with private funding. Inside the park, he recommended removing a number of facilities and replacing the ballfield, grandstand,

and eagle cage in the upper park with an open lawn, as intended in the park's plan. He also suggested an irregular shoreline for the island being built in Green Lake. In response to the growing number of vehicles in the city, he recommended adding a parking lot between the island area and the wooded portion of the park just uphill from shore and developing a walk around the lake, as funding allowed. At Jefferson Park, Dawson directed the planting of trees and shrubs in a naturalistic arrangement to block the views of the houses. He criticized the planting on the west side of the park as too flat and ordered. He thought the western border planting should include native trees and shrubs, while the eastern border should be planted with low-growing trees such as dogwoods, hawthorns, and flowering crab apples. He made few suggestions about Seward Park, mostly focusing on the walks along Lake Washington Boulevard near the park entrance. The park board did not record any comments on Dawson's report in its meeting minutes, and a decade would pass before they would request further plans or advice from the firm.

When John Olmsted died in 1920, Seattle newspapers ran notices of his death, although they are somewhat more perfunctory than might be expected for someone who had such a tremendous impact on the city and who worked with so many of the most prominent citizens. This may be attributed to his reserved demeanor, something he mentioned himself several times in his letters to Sophie. He was described by Elbert Blaine during his first visit, in 1903, as someone who "possesses a personality that

Kroll Map Company's 1920 map of Seattle's park and boulevard system showing the extent of the Olmsted park system that had been developed.

WHEREAS the Divine Ruler of the Universe has in His infinite wisdom taken from his home and family John C. Olmstead, and

WHEREAS the Board of Park Commissioners of the City of Seattle, through intimate personal and business relations with him, realize that the members of his family have suffered the loss of a devoted and loving husband, and a considerate affectionate father, and

WHEREAS through the years of laying out and developing of the Park and Boulevard system of this City under his skillful and able management, he has endeared himself to all who were associated with him; therefore be it

RESOLVED that the Board of Park Commissioners of the City of Seattle extend to the members of the bereaved family its deep and sincere condolence and sympathy in this, the hour of their great loss; trusting that their abiding faith in Him who doeth all things well may soften their grief with love.

(Adopted by the Board of Park Commissioners on March 5, 1920.)

grows upon one as it unfolds itself. He is such an unassuming man that at first glance he might leave a tendency to disappointment, but this quickly fades away as one watches him at work, associates with him and meets him under the conditions in which the park board has been his associates for several days past."

A remembrance by Emanuel T. Mische, a landscape architect who had worked with the Olmsted Brothers firm as a park superintendent in Portland, Oregon, published in the April 1920 issue of *Parks and Recreation*, was more personal and praised Olmsted, writing, "The range of difficulties he solved in city planning would in itself be a creditable record but this he did as a by product in the planning of the country's pleasureways, parks and playgrounds."

In 1928, when Albert S. Kerry, a former private client of the firm, became park board chairman, Charles Saunders, then serving as a state representative, again lobbied for the commissioners to hire the Olmsted Brothers. Dawson and Kerry exchanged cordial letters. Kerry explained his frustration with the city council authorizing purchases of parkland outside the city limits (Carkeek Park and Matthews Beach) and his desire to hire the Olmsted Brothers firm to prepare a new comprehensive plan to guide park development and acquisitions. He also asked if Dawson had any of the plans prepared for the Seattle parks, as they could find only some of them in the Park Department's files.

The letters between Kerry and Dawson continued for the better part of a year, but none of

Control of the Park Department would remain a contentious issue over the ensuing decades. In 1967, a city charter amendment made the park board an advisory body, renamed the Park Department the Department of Parks and Recreation, and shifted control to the mayor and city council and the park superintendent. This arrangement persisted until voters formed the metropolitan park district in 2014, which designated the city council as the park district governing board and established a park levy to fund the department separately from the city's general budget.

The beach at Carkeek Park in northwest Seattle.

Kerry's efforts to get the park board on solid ground or to hire the Olmsted Brothers succeeded. The city council refused to allocate funding for hiring the firm. The relationship between the city council and park board would deteriorate further when the park board used the initiative process to get a measure on the March 1929 ballot to establish a metropolitan park district. Forming a park district would have severed most of the city council's oversight and involvement in the park system. Dawson reviewed Kerry's public messages about the measure and provided feedback and helpful information from other park systems around the country. The initiative failed, however, and the correspondence between the two men ended.

After the failure of the 1929 ballot measure, there remained one more significant public project for the Olmsted Brothers in Seattle. Over his years working in Seattle, Dawson formed a number of personal relationships with local residents, particularly those who had hired the firm to design landscape plans for their homes. One of these friends was Sophie Krauss, who with her husband, Arthur, owned the home known as Firworthy, located on Lake Washington Boulevard in the Denny-Blaine neighborhood. Krauss was a member of the Seattle Garden Club, one of the groups working on developing an arboretum in Washington Park that would be jointly operated by the Park Department and the University of Washington.

There was very little funding for park development in the budget of either the park board or the university to actually create the arboretum. In 1933, Seattle Garden Club member Edna Grinstead approached Hugo Winkenwerder, dean of the College of Forestry and acting president of the University of Washington, to develop a plan to move the arboretum project forward. Winkenwerder; Grinstead and her husband, Loren, an attorney; Herbert Ihrig, a local

Members of the Seattle Garden Club in about 1930, likely at the University of Washington.

Firworthy, the Krauss home landscape designed by the Olmsted Brothers, primarily through the work of Fred Dawson in the late 1920s and early 1930s.

horticulture enthusiast; Lee Paul Sieg, soon to be the university's president; and Sophie Krauss met to discuss it.

Loren Grinstead served on the state unemployment relief committee, and the arboretum project qualified for funding through the Works Progress Administration. The funds could only be used for labor associated with construction of the arboretum, but the workers needed a plan to guide their work. The park board did not have any funds available to hire a landscape architect, but as Charles Saunders would report in a letter, Sophie Krauss told those gathered that Dawson was a "man whose work

Fred Dawson completed the arboretum plan by March 1936, just four months after he received the topographical maps from the city. He rushed the planning to keep up with the workers being paid with relief funds who had already begun to clear land for development. He wanted to ensure they did not remove any vegetation that would be needed for the arboretum plan. In a departure from the system used by the Arnold Arboretum, but in keeping with the practice of other arboretums developed at the time, Dawson chose to organize the plant groups according to a taxonomic system developed by Adolf Engler and Karl Prantl in 1887, which organized plants according to their ancestral relationships to other plants. Dawson adjusted the Engler and Prantl system somewhat to accommodate conditions on the ground.

At the north end of the park, Dawson laid out a series of lagoons that would be created by dredging. They would bring water views into the park, as John Olmsted had recommended in his 1904 plan. Dawson placed a rock garden on the hillside along the eastern ridge around an existing creek, which he reconstructed into a series of ponds and falls as it traveled downhill. Dawson also planned a similar treatment for Arboretum Creek. The open meadows along that creek were kept open, with plantings of different species from the Oleaceae (lilac) family.

Dawson also made plans for the park's structures. He added a second road, Arboretum Drive, along the east side to increase access to that area of the park and placed administrative buildings at the northern entrance to the park. He put the service buildings along an existing access road to the gated Broadmoor community.

One highlight of the park would be Azalea Way, a turf path bordered by Japanese cherry trees and eastern dogwoods and an undergrowth of azaleas. The development of Azalea Way would require more than 10,000 hours of hand labor and 500 railroad cars of compost. When it was completed in 1940, crews had planted 500 trees and 2,100 azaleas. In 1937, Dawson predicted, "When this planting is carried out it cannot help but be the most magnificent display of this sort in the world."

Azalea Way bursts with color each spring when the thousands of azaleas that line the path bloom.

Hugo Winkenwerder, University of Washington dean, shown here at Pack Forest in Pierce County in about 1930, played a key role in developing the Washington Park Arboretum after years of failed attempts to establish an arboretum on the grounds of the university.

was familiar to many of our residents[,] was a regular visitor to the northwest[,] and whose knowledge of this work would be of value." Additionally, the Olmsted Brothers firm, and its predecessor Olmsted firms, had designed a number of arboreta, including Frederick Law Olmsted Sr.'s work on Harvard's Arnold Arboretum. Dawson had grown up in the Arnold Arboretum because his father, Jackson Thornton Dawson, had been the head plantsman and superintendent there for 43 years. To bridge the gap in funding, the Seattle Garden Club agreed to pay for Dawson's services in designing the arboretum.

Besides the Washington Park project, very little of the Olmsted Brothers plans were developed in the city during the Great Depression. Instead, the pressures of the growing city began intruding on the parks, with a dire consequence for Woodland Park. The bisecting roadway that Olmsted had deflected in 1908 reemerged in 1930 as the new path for the Pacific Highway (today's State Route 99), the route running north and south through Western Washington. At that time, the state highway ran along existing city streets once it entered the city at North 85th Street, but along with construction of the George Washington Memorial Bridge (more commonly known as the Aurora Bridge), the city and the state Highway Department wanted to develop a more direct route through the northern part of the city. Much as the earlier discussion about the traffic roadway through the park stemmed from a desire to travel to the north side of Green Lake as directly as possible from the Stone Avenue Bridge, the new alignment was related to a desire to travel directly north from the Aurora Bridge site. This had been chosen for a variety of technical reasons, but primarily because it allowed the bridge to meet the Army Corps of Engineers' height requirements for a fixed span across the Lake Washington Ship Canal.

Unfortunately, the routing brought a six-lane highway plus two sidewalks right through the center of Woodland Park. The plan called for pedestrian overpasses to bridge the gap in the park created by the highway, but there was no denying the discontinuity

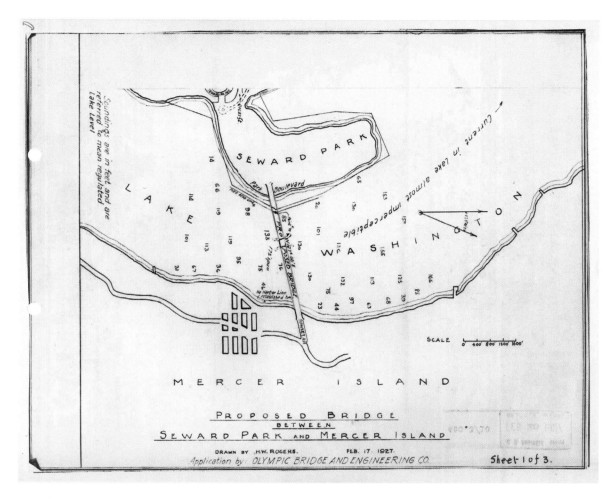

Aurora Avenue, U. S. Route 99 through North Seattle shown here in 1936, sliced through the middle of Woodland Park when it was built in the early 1930s.

Map showing a bridge extending from the park boulevard in Seward Park to Mercer Island that was proposed in 1927. The project would later be abandoned in favor of the Lake Washington Floating Bridge, which would open in 1940.

it would bring to the park experience and the loss of parkland the project would entail. Opponents of the project carried out a campaign to sway voters, but when the issue came to a vote on November 4, 1930, the referendum failed and the project moved forward.

A similarly destructive proposal for Seward Park emerged in 1927. State highway planners located the approach to a bridge to carry traffic from Seattle to Mercer Island in Seward Park. That potential intrusion and loss of parkland would not be resolved until 1938, when the bridge project was moved to the Mount Baker neighborhood.

A third transportation project threatening parks and boulevards was the routing of Empire Expressway

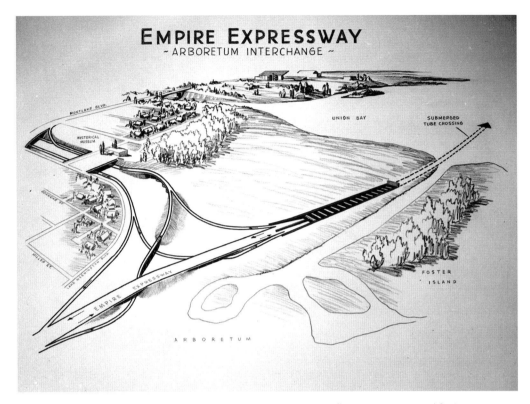

EMPIRE EXPRESSWAY
~ ARBORETUM INTERCHANGE ~

When plans for the Empire Expressway (later renamed the R. H. Thomson Expressway) began developing in the 1950s, a major interchange between the expressway and the planned Evergreen Point Floating Bridge was located in Washington Park. The project would have involved the loss of parkland and would have negatively impacted a significant portion of the remaining park.

(later renamed the R. H. Thomson Expressway) through the Rainier Valley, the Central District, Washington Park, and neighborhoods north of the ship canal. This idea had been bandied about for several decades and would eventually involve loss of parkland for the ramps that would have connected the expressway with the Evergreen Point Bridge. The expressway would be stopped in the 1960s by public outcry led by the Citizens Against the R. H. Thomson and a coalition of community groups, including the Black Panthers. The ramps will all be removed as part of the Evergreen Point Bridge reconstruction project, restoring parkland and protecting the character of Lake Washington Boulevard.

After World War II, Seattle and King County had to catch up with the growth spurt they had experienced with the arrival of workers for the region's wartime industries. In 1951, the King County Planning Commission formed the Puget Sound Study Group to assess how the Olmsted Brothers plans and Bogue's *Plan of Seattle* for open space could be further realized. The resulting vision could be succinctly summarized as "more land, now." They credited Olmsted for what parkland the city had and declared:

The Time to Make the Long Range Plan is Now!
To meet the Public Need, we should

- *Secure and develop public waterfront*

- *Preserve forest areas as parks*

- *Provide space for playgrounds, games and sports*

- *Maintain a system of parkways for easy access to beaches and parks*

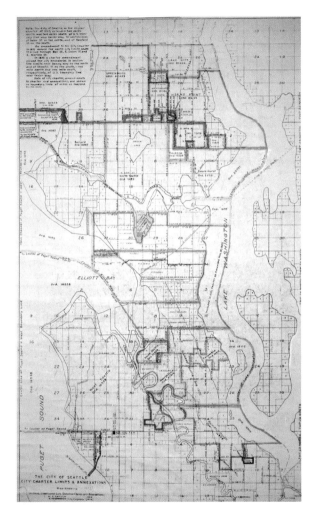

In the 1950s, large swaths of north Seattle, north and east of Green Lake, were annexed to the city. It was the first significant growth of the city's land mass since the series of annexations that occurred between 1906 and 1910. The Board of Park Commissioners did not commission a new supplemental park system plan as they had for the earlier annexations, and acquisition and development of park facilities in this part of the city has been more ad hoc than it has been elsewhere.

But as park superintendent Paul V. Brown would write in his 1956 annual report, this was an "era of disappointments and failures," including four failed park bond measures and very little parkland acquisition. The need for open space was amplified when annexations in 1954 brought the area between North 85th Street and North 145th Street, from Lake Washington to Puget Sound, into the city. Much of this land had been subdivided and developed already, but just a handful of significant parks (Jackson Park, Matthews Beach, and Carkeek Park) had been incorporated into the new residential areas.

The next big spurt of parkland acquisition and development would not come until the 1970s, after the Forward Thrust park bond measure was passed by King County voters in February 1968. It would lead to tremendous growth in suburban parks throughout the county. In Seattle, the bonds addressed some of the undeveloped parts of the 1903 and 1908 Olmsted plans as well as areas not originally incorporated into the plans. The funding assisted in the development of a number of parks recommended in those plans, most notably Gas Works Park on Lake Union and Discovery Park in Magnolia.

At the same time that the city was expanding its parkland, a parallel movement emerged to preserve and restore its historic parks and parkways. Across the United States, a movement to preserve historic architecture had grown to national prominence in the 1960s. Before long, an understanding of the need to preserve and protect cultural landscapes developed, beginning with the most iconic Olmsted landscapes. In New York City, Central Park was landmarked in 1963, followed by Prospect Park in 1975. The same

Myrtle Edwards Park, developed in the 1970s, realized Olmsted's vision for a waterfront park at the northern end of the harbor. It runs along the shore between the Olympic Sculpture Park, opened in 2007, and Centennial Park, which opened in 1974.

pattern emerged in Seattle, with Pioneer Square and Pike Place Market designated as historic districts in 1970 and 1971, respectively, to protect their historic buildings, but the value of the local Olmsted parks and parkways was not yet widely recognized.

While Seattle Parks and Recreation employees were aware of the city's Olmsted legacy, it was not formally identified as a historic resource until a series of events led to national recognition of Seattle's park and boulevard system. The process began with a letter from an Erie County official in Buffalo, New York, to the Junior League of Seattle, sent in about 1977. The letter has been lost to time, but Donald Harris, who was then the director of the capital improvement program at Parks and Recreation, remembers that a Buffalo group was forming to protect and restore their Olmsted & Vaux-designed park system, the first public park system in the United States. Although it had been altered by urban developments and neglect, it was largely intact. Harris recalls that the organizers, who would establish the Buffalo Friends of Olmsted Parks in 1978, saw parallels between the Buffalo and Seattle park systems, so they reached out to Seattle as part of their effort to build a network of people interested in Olmsted parks across the country.

The letter appears to have spurred the Junior League of Seattle to action. They shared the letter with Department of Parks and Recreation Superintendent Walter Hundley. Hundley, who had a background as a pastor, Model Cities program director, and budget director for the City of Seattle, not as a landscape architect, was immediately interested in the issue, and he joined with University of Washington landscape architecture professor David Streatfield to write articles for the October 1979 issue of the Junior League's publication, *Puget Soundings*, on the history and future of the park system. In a related development that same year, Seattle's Office of Urban Conservation, a predecessor of today's Historic Preservation program in the Department of Neighborhoods, created an exhibit about Seattle's Olmsted heritage. It was displayed as part of an annual series of programs hosted at the downtown Nordstrom store to celebrate Seattle.

Hundley and Harris traveled to Buffalo in May 1980 for the Olmsted conference hosted by the Buffalo Friends of Olmsted Parks. They learned about the larger context and historical significance of the Olmsted park system in Seattle and returned with a vision to restore and protect Seattle's Olmsted landscapes. At the same meeting, the participants formed the National Association for Olmsted Parks to increase awareness of the Olmsted firms and their work, which extended over more than a century, from Olmsted & Vaux, formed in 1857, to the Olmsted Associates, which had just closed in 1979.

At that time, Olmsted-related history and design principles were studied by students in landscape architecture programs at universities, and many of the Olmstedian principles still guided landscape architects' work, as they continue to do today. Donald Harris remembers Seattle landscape architect Rich Untermann recommending in 1976 that park planners working on the Genesee Park and Playfield project

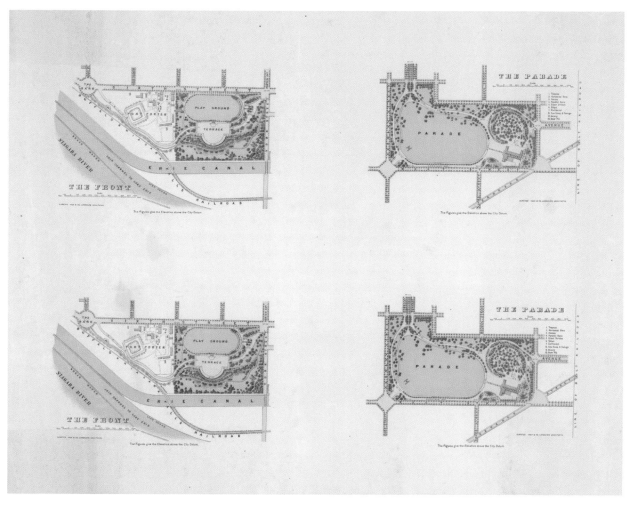

Reproductions of plans made for Buffalo, New York's park system, including "The Front" and "The Parade."

delve into the Olmsted history of Lake Washington Boulevard and integrate the new park into the existing Olmsted system and incorporate its design principles. Similarly, Rae Tufts, former planner with the Department of Parks and Recreation, remembers referencing the Olmsted vision for the park and boulevard system in her work in the 1970s.

Although landscape architecture professionals certainly understood and valued the system's import, public awareness of the Olmsted Brothers' work in

SEATTLE PUBLIC LIBRARY

SEATTLE PUBLIC LIBRARY
SEP 15 1977

Seattle
Preservation Handbook

R
MNGP

The Office of Urban Conservation developed Seattle's first historic preservation guidelines, outlined in this handbook from 1977. The office became the Department of Neighborhoods' Historic Preservation Program in 1992. Its staff has worked with the Department of Parks and Recreation and community groups to protect Olmsted Brothers-designed landscapes in Seattle.

Seattle and on the West Coast and its significance faded between the 1930s and 1970s. The *Olmsted* park system regularly touted on city maps, in magazine and newspaper articles, and in real estate advertisements in the 1910s and 1920s became the *Seattle* park system. As such, these parks and parkways were important parts of people's lives. Neighborhoods that were built around the parks identified strongly with those landscapes. The parks, playfields, playgrounds, boulevards, and parkways, and their vistas, plantings, forests, and facilities shaped the character of the city and were beloved, but their historical significance and the need to protect and preserve them as historic landscapes were not well defined in the public mind.

When Hundley and Harris returned from Buffalo, it was apparent to them that a significant part of the Seattle park system's effectiveness in serving the city was due to the Olmsted Brothers' influence. To retain the characteristics Olmsted built into the landscape and park system designs, Hundley and Harris realized, the department would have to invest in restoring, preserving, and protecting the system's historical character. Looking to the efforts underway in the eastern states, they decided to engage with the public to develop awareness of Seattle's remarkable park system and its history and to find others interested in getting involved. In June 1981, the department hosted a program called "A Seattle Legacy: The Olmsted Parks" with the Washington Chapter of the American Society of Landscape Architects at the Museum of History and Industry.

It featured a talk by the executive director of the National Association for Olmsted Parks, Alexander W. Allport. The Department of Parks and Recreation hoped to draw at least a handful of interested people. To their surprise, 160 people attended the talk. Given that it was clearly the park system that drew the crowd (they would not have known of Allport personally), Harris remembers thinking, "Aha! We have a constituency." Out of that event, a core group came together. They formed the Friends of Seattle's Olmsted Parks (FSOP) at a meeting on November 17, 1981, in the Woodland Park Zoo's activity resource center. The group officially incorporated in 1983, and described themselves as "committed to education of the public about our Olmsted Park design heritage and our legacy of other public and private Olmsted landscape designs."

Working closely with the Department of Parks and Recreation, FSOP began a multi-pronged effort to raise awareness and restore and protect the landscapes that continues today. They cohosted a community celebration of Seattle's Olmsted legacy with the Department of Parks and Recreation and Board of Park Commissioners at Hiawatha Playfield on May 31, 1984. The following September, the group's first large event was a national Olmsted conference with the theme "Olmsted Parks of the West: The Future of a Tradition." FSOP partnered with the Seattle Department of Parks and Recreation, the University of Washington, the Seattle Chapter of the American Society of Landscape Architects, the National Association for Olmsted Parks, and others to

SEATTLE OLMSTED LEGACY CELEBRATION
Hiawatha Community Center
Thursday, May 31, 1984
7:30 p.m.

Program from the 1984 centennial of the Seattle park department celebration at Hiawatha Playfield.

hold the conference. Activities included a reception, a guided tour of the Olmsted-designed Highlands community, and a tour of Seattle's Olmsted parks (in advance of the tour, Donald Harris spearheaded an effort to restore the original Olmsted-era bridge balustrade in Frink Park, which had been damaged and replaced with a generic steel guardrail). An exhibit at the Museum of History and Industry, "Art of the Olmsted Landscape," opened on the same day as the conference.

In 1984, voters approved a series of bond measures for infrastructure improvements across the city that came to be known as the Seattle 1-2-3 measures. The park measure funded a range of maintenance projects, and the Department of Parks and Recreation wanted to use some of the funding to invest in Lake Washington Boulevard—but planners

realized they needed to know what restoration of the historic boulevard should look like before they began work. They hired EDAW, Inc., and Walmsley & Co., Inc., two landscape architecture and urban planning firms, to complete an assessment of the boulevard and provide recommendations for its restoration. The resulting report marked an important shift in thinking about Seattle's Olmsted park system. For the first time, the Department of Parks and Recreation officially recognized the need to manage Olmsted landscapes as historical resources, in addition to being elements of the city's park system.

The interplay, and in some cases tension, between those two identities has been the focus of collaborative efforts over the subsequent decades as Parks staff, Friends of Seattle's Olmsted Parks members, and neighborhood park supporters have worked to restore and protect the Olmsted park and boulevard system. The challenges include the demands of maintenance—labor-intensive planting beds, aging trees, invasive-plant eradication, aging structures, and more demand for use-specific spaces in parks—and encroachments, which result when private property owners' landscaping, retaining walls, driveways, and even, in at least one case, a swimming pool, creep into park boulevard rights-of-way or parks. This causes a disruption in the landscapes' intended character and a loss of public use of those spaces. A particular challenge is the lack of adequate budgets to maintain historic structures and planting beds.

Beyond the challenges within the system, the integrity of the whole is challenged by projects and

Olmsted Historic Landscapes Act

One of the initiatives that emerged out of the formation of the National Association for Olmsted Parks was the introduction of the Olmsted Historic Landscapes Act in 1984. The act would have launched a nationwide inventory of Olmsted landscapes as the first step in assessing their impact on American communities and developing plans for the preservation and maintenance of them under the auspices of the National Park Service. Seattle Parks and Recreation's Donald Harris traveled to Washington, D.C., to testify on behalf of the bill, and the measure passed the House of Representatives, but not the Senate. The work of identifying, protecting, restoring, and promoting awareness of Olmsted landscapes has continued, however, with the work of the National Association for Olmsted Parks and numerous local organizations.

Seattle Public Utilities placed its new combined sewer overflow tank under the tennis courts at Seward Park. The project involved reconstruction of the tennis courts, shoreline improvements, and reclamation of the southernmost portion of the park, which had been largely inaccessible to park users prior to the project. As a result, a significant environmental-protection facility could be built in the best place for its requirements while also benefiting the park and its users.

developments in the city. As population density, demand for multi-modal transportation networks, and utility infrastructure have increased, open space in parks and along boulevards has often been seen as publicly owned "empty space" that can be used to meet these new demands. Sometimes designs can be developed to benefit both the parkland and the public projects, but often a net loss of parkland or loss of historic landscape character results.

The efforts to meet the challenges of maintaining a cultural landscape that is also an integral part of an urban environment have also involved educational programs. In 1987, Friends of Seattle's Olmsted Parks

members developed a six-projector slide show on the Olmsted vision for the park and boulevard system. At Superintendent Hundley's request this was shown to all 900 park employees. Ten years later, FSOP installed six interpretive panels in the Volunteer Park water tower's observation level and developed the first of four topical pamphlets on Olmsted cultural landscapes in Washington.

The Friends of Seattle's Olmsted Parks also took on a major project to gather the primary sources related to the 1903 and 1908 plans and the plans for individual landscapes. These documents and plans could only be accessed at the Frederick Law

NATIONAL ASSOCIATION FOR OLMSTED PARKS

DECLARATION

May 3, 2003   Seattle, Washington

     The National Association for Olmsted Parks recognizes, in this Centennial Celebration Year, the wisdom of Seattle's early leaders in bringing John Charles Olmsted to the city to design and implement an outstanding system of parks, parkways and boulevards.

     This system, executed between 1903 and 1938 is nationally significant – so innovative was the Olmsted vision for this interconnected system, that it represents, nationally, the first attempt to "borrow" landscape scenery on a grand and monumental scale. As a precursor to the California State Park System, 1929, the Seattle Olmsted legacy is a pioneering masterwork and a potential candidate for a National Historic Landmark – the highest honor that can be bestowed on a historic property in America.

     Today, as we congregate in Volunteer Park, we can not only witness the integrity and contiguity of Olmsted's vision but we can also experience the "passages of scenery" intended by the Master. For example, this park contains such integrated landscape features as the reservoir, which sill reflects its landscape surrounding and mirrors the overhead sky; and the sentinel water tower, providing a beacon and a welcoming invitation to Seattleites one hundred years later. Thank you city fathers and J. C. Olmsted for providing us with such a rare and regionally unique legacy.

In honor of the Olmsted Brothers' park system centennial, the National Association for Olmsted Parks made a declaration on May 3, 2003.

National Association for Olmsted Parks Conference at the old Naval Reserve Armory (now MOHAI) in South Lake Union, held in Seattle in honor of the park system centennial.

Olmsted National Historic Site (at Fairsted) in Brookline, Massachusetts, at the Library of Congress in Washington, D.C., or at the Loeb Library at Harvard University. Miscellaneous correspondence and related documents were in local repositories, such as the Seattle Municipal Archives, Special Collections at the University of Washington Libraries, and the Seattle Public Library's Seattle Room. FSOP researched the history of the parks and boulevards and compiled notebooks of reference materials, which would become useful for documenting and preserving the legacy of the Olmsted firm in Seattle and the region. Later projects, some funded as mitigation for transportation project impacts on park properties, have made many of these materials available online.

In 2003, the Friends of Seattle's Olmsted Parks developed a yearlong program to celebrate the centennial of Olmsted's first Seattle park and boulevard system plan. The centerpiece for the year was hosting a second national conference, "Our Olmsted Legacy: Learning from the Past, Inspiring the Future," which coincided with the annual meeting of the National Association for Olmsted Parks. FSOP partnered with 45 organizations throughout the year to offer public programs to celebrate and highlight what the Olmsted legacy means to Seattle. FSOP encouraged partners to incorporate some aspect of the Olmsted legacy in their own annual programs.

One of the most significant results was the shift in how the Cascade Land Conservancy (now Forterra) approached their strategic planning. Inspired by the 100-year vision that Olmsted provided for Seattle and its park system in 1903, Forterra's president, Gene Duvernoy, saw the wisdom of using a 100-

year framework when planning the future of the city and region. Fifteen years later, this continued to be a guiding strategy for Forterra's work, and in 2018, Forterra was awarded the prestigious Olmsted Medal by the American Society of Landscape Architects at its national conference. The nomination quoted a statement from Forterra's website that illustrated how the organization embodies Olmstedian ideals: "The interconnectedness of the natural, built and now the social world is key to unlocking solutions to a resilient region. To save nature we must solve human problems. Through the prism of land, Forterra is committed to addressing the quality of the underlying social fabric that binds us. This place is who we are."

The Friends of Seattle's Olmsted Parks, when partnering with the Seattle Department of Parks and Recreation, has also advocated looking forward to the next century. The 2000 Pro Parks levy allocated $198.2 million for upgrades to existing parks and acquisition of new parks. It was the biggest increase in the park system since the Olmsted plan-related acquisitions of the early 20th century. It represented an extension of that original planning to ensure the park system would serve the ever-growing population and those areas that had not been part of the city when the original park system was laid out, particularly the northern reaches of the city.

As park use has changed, the Department of Parks and Recreation and other agencies have developed new plans for parkland that are informed by the Olmsted designs and intentions for them, but also accommodate changing circumstances. One such project was the redevelopment of Lincoln Reservoir and the adjacent Bobby Morris Playfield (the

Delridge Playfield (Youngstown Playfield).

Cal Anderson Park's redevelopment, completed in 2005, adapted the Olmsted plan for the park to new conditions created by the need to place the city water reservoir underground.

combined area renamed Cal Anderson Park in 2003) when Seattle Public Utilities began work to place the reservoir in the park underground for water safety in 2002. The Friends of Seattle's Olmsted Parks and a neighborhood community group, Groundswell Off Broadway, lobbied for a new park design that would incorporate Olmsted's vision for the park and open up the area on top of the reservoir to public use.

Working with Seattle Parks and Recreation, Seattle Public Utilities, the city Landmarks Preservation Board, and the landscape architecture firm Berger Partnership, the community helped ensure that the park plan evoked the historic park and its Olmsted design intent. A fountain and reflecting pool on top of the underground reservoir retained a water feature in the park. Sections of the original reservoir balustrade were left in place adjacent to the gatehouse, and replicated sections were placed at the other three corners of the original reservoir's location. Corner planting beds were restored and trees added that sustained Olmsted's idea that the park should have a wide variety of tree species, for year-round seasonal interest. Other improvements in the park as part of the project included renovated playfields and the removal of fencing directly adjacent to the sidewalks near the ballfields. New planting beds along the sidewalks and less conspicuous fencing strengthened the connection between the neighborhood and the park.

Similar efforts to combine renovations with the historical intent of the park designs have been carried out at Jefferson Park, Woodland Park Zoo, the Washington Park Arboretum, and others. As a result of these types of projects, the century-old parks are more sustainable, are better adapted to new uses, and still retain their essential Olmsted character and their roles in the park and boulevard system.

Looking ahead, Seattle's Olmsted parks and boulevards face numerous challenges as the city grows, the climate changes, and patterns of use shift with changing recreation needs and transportation modes. Even with the addition of parks and green spaces over the past 40 years, the population increase in the current burst of growth has put a strain on the park system. Parks face the danger of being "loved to death," especially in the face of shortfalls in the maintenance budget.

The very nature of historic landscapes makes them ever-changing, and they need different management than buildings to maintain their historic integrity and preserve the experience they are intended to provide. Vegetation grows and ages, requiring tending and replacement. Trees are particularly challenging because removing even one aging tree has a large impact on park users' experiences. In Seattle's parks that were developed a century ago, large numbers of trees will need to be replaced in a process that will have to be managed

carefully to preserve the intent of the Olmsted design. In view corridors, particularly those from hillsides with vegetation below the line of sight, which are key elements of Olmsted's designs and his vision for the park system, vegetation needs to be managed so it does not grow up and block the intended view. This is particularly problematic where "volunteer" tree seeds have taken root in unintended places. Those trees then grow into the views, but removing them is costly and can run afoul of the city's urban forest policies.

Vegetation management in the face of climate change poses additional issues. As rainfall and temperature patterns change, tree and plant species that have long flourished in Seattle are struggling to adapt. At the same time, plant pathogens that thrive in the new conditions further weaken them. These changes are affecting all types of vegetation, from ferns to western red cedars. Protecting the tree canopy and the woodland character of landscapes like Seward or Schmitz Parks will take careful management.

The built environment in Seattle parks and boulevards is also feeling the pressure of population growth and changing use patterns. Olmsted could never have envisioned the volume and impact of motor vehicles and the safety infrastructure they require. Lake Washington Boulevard was long-protected from commercial traffic by its status as a park boulevard, but in 1951, the city changed the traffic code, and the boulevards and parkways became part of the city's general street system. This opened them up to more traffic and put the street portion of the right-of-way under the control of the Engineering Department. Along with the increased traffic, this change has also necessitated alterations to the

Just as Olmsted predicted, groves of old trees have become vanishingly rare in the environs of Seattle, and there are few places where residents can wander among towering cedars, like the one in Seward Park shown here, without traveling far beyond the city limits.

Jefferson Park, another Olmsted park redesigned to accommodate the placing of its water reservoir underground. The redesigned park opened in 2012 and incorporated elements from the original Olmsted plan, particularly its circulation routes and emphasis on views outside the park toward the city, the bay, and the distant mountains.

infrastructure of the streets, including the addition of curbs and safety features, which can detract from the park experience on the drives.

Despite these challenges, Seattle's Olmsted park and boulevard system continues to be one of the defining features of the city. The vision that Olmsted laid out in his park plans has largely been realized. The parkways and boulevards nearly encircle the city, albeit with some gaps. They extend parkland into the neighborhoods outside the parks proper and provide pedestrians, bicyclists, and vehicular traffic with parklike experiences as they move about the

city. The drives range in character from more formal neighborhood drives in Montlake and Mount Baker to informal, wooded drives like Interlaken and Cheasty. Threading their way through forests and along shorelines, they provide access to some of the best views in the city.

As Olmsted intended, the large parks around the city all have unique characters that are shaped by their particular natural assets. Walking along the path encircling Seward Park, visitors can view a panorama of mountains from Mount Baker to Mount Rainier, with the lake in the foreground. The park's

Glimpses of stunning water and mountain views such as this one through the trees in Discovery Park explain Olmsted's desire to incorporate the military fort into the city's park system. It is these large, publicly owned spaces that provide access for all of the city's residents to the region's spectacular landscapes and the benefits they provide for people's health and happiness.

interior paths wind through a dense forest of cedars, firs, maples, ferns, and salal. Woodland Park has a forested midsection along its eastern slope flanked by recreational facilities on the east and zoological gardens on the west. Green Lake's footpath encircles one of the city's smaller lakes, with views across the water providing glimpses of tree groves and fringes of shoreline vegetation. Alki Beach preserves a long stretch of saltwater shoreline for public access, with views across the sound and back toward the city, as well as a walkway and bicycle path along its length. Washington Park is home to the arboretum, jointly

View across Lake Washington southeast of Seward Park, 2015. As Olmsted envisioned, the park is prized by the community for shoreline views and water recreation and its forest trails.

Woodland Park has undergone a number of alterations since Olmsted developed its preliminary plan. The Rose Garden, however, can be found on the preliminary plan from 1910, where Olmsted placed a formal flower garden with a geometric grid of paths.

operated by Seattle Parks and Recreation and the University of Washington; the Japanese Garden, jointly managed by the city and the Arboretum Foundation; and trails through its wooded interior. Jefferson Park's perch at the edge of Beacon Hill provides vistas of downtown, the sound, and the Olympic Mountains, as well as a public golf course, while Volunteer Park captures the view north of downtown that includes the sound, the mountains, and the Space Needle. Volunteer Park also has a distinct character as the most formally designed of the Olmsted parks.

Beyond the iconic landscapes, the playgrounds, playfields, and neighborhood parks developed out of the Olmsted Brothers' plans—whether recommended for inclusion in the park system, influenced by the Olmsted Brothers' advice, or designed by Olmsted or one of his associates—

have created a richly textured tapestry of open space for the city's residents. The Olmsted system parks and parkways are vital elements of neighborhood livability and identity. They are gathering places for residents of all ages and home to community centers that offer a wide variety of programs.

Olmsted's park and boulevard system has shaped where and how people live in Seattle, and how people experience the city. Where there might have been a simple grid of streets, there are sweeping park boulevards that wind through forests and along shorelines. Where development could have claimed areas of natural beauty entirely for private use, the parks make a wide variety of landscapes available to everyone. And, at a seminal moment in Seattle's history, civic leaders established a tradition of far-sighted planning for public open space and embraced the Olmsted ideal of beautiful refuges from city life together with places for active recreation well distributed and available to all for the benefit of the whole. That vision has become part of how the city defines itself and will undoubtedly continue to serve as the foundation for Seattle's park system far into the future.

SEATTLE'S OLMSTED PARK SYSTEM

The list of parks that make up Seattle's Olmsted park and boulevard system is extensive. In addition to the 1903 and 1908 system plans and the 1910 playgrounds report, John Olmsted, Fred Dawson, and, to a very limited extent, Rick Olmsted, provided designs for parks, boulevards, and playfields, and consulted with the Board of Park Commissioners and private developers on the location and layout of parks and boulevards. Additionally, a number of their recommendations were realized in parkland acquired more than a half-century later.

The list below includes all of the public landscapes the firm recommended for Seattle in their plans or correspondence, designed, or helped shape through their advice. References to them can be found in the system plans, the 1910 playgrounds report, and other correspondence. Additionally, the landscapes marked with a ❋ have correspondence related to their design, location, or function that can be found in the Library of Congress records available via the Washington State Digital Archives, at the Seattle Municipal Archives, or at the University of Washington Special Collections. Those marked with a ✥ have landscape plans from the Frederick Law Olmsted National Historic Site. Links to the correspondence and plans are available via the National Association for Olmsted Parks' *OlmstedOnline.org* using job number 02690 (Seattle Park System) or the number listed with each location. The Seattle Park System (02690) files have information regarding the park system and some of the individual parks and boulevards. The files also contain documents pertaining to landscapes without specific job numbers.

Names used by the Olmsted Brothers or the Board of Park Commissioners, but since changed, are noted in parentheses.

Alki Beach Park (02716)✳ ❧

Alki Playground

Bagley Viewpoint (see 02713)

Ballard Playground (Parker Playfield)

Beacon Avenue (see 02725)✳ ❧ Beacon Playground
(Beacon Hill Playfield)

Beer Sheva Park (Atlantic City Addition Park)

Boren Park (formerly part of Interlaken Park)

Brighton Playfield (sited near recommended
location for Graham Avenue Playfield)

Cal Anderson Park (02691)✳ ❧ (Lincoln Park)

Carkeek Drive (portion of proposed Dunlap Parkway)

Cascade Playground (Pontius Park)

Cheasty Boulevard (see 02725)

Coe Play Park (North Queen Anne Playground)

Cowen Park (02707)✳ ❧

David Rodgers Park (design recommendations for
existing municipally owned land in 1903 report)

Dearborn Park (Somerville Park)

Delridge Playfield (Youngstown Playfield)

Denny-Blaine Park (pre-existing park located
adjacent to boulevard)

Denny Park (02704)✳ (park predates
Olmsted planning)

Discovery Park (02720)✳ ❧ (Fort Lawton)

East Montlake Park (02711)

Frink Park (02708)✳ ❧

Garfield Playfield

Georgetown Playfield (Duwamish River Park)

Gilman Playground (Market Street Playfield)

Golden Gardens Park (03348)✳

Green Lake Park (02714)✳ ❧
(Green Lake Boulevard)✳ ❧

Greenwood Triangle✳ (portion of Ballard Parkway)

Hamilton Viewpoint Park (portion of
Duwamish Head Park)

Hiawatha Playfield (02715)✳ ❧
(West Seattle Playfield)

Hunter Boulevard (03209)✳ ❧

Interbay Athletic Complex (Interbay Park)

Interlaken Park (02713, see also 02717)✳ ❧
(Interlaken Boulevard)

Jefferson Park (02725)✳ ❧

Kinnear Park (02692)✳ ❧

Lake Park Drive (see 03209)

Lake Washington Boulevard (02718, also see 02699,
02708, 02721, 02724, 03209, 07315)✳

Lakeview Park✳

Lakewood Triangle✳ (see 03209)

Landing Parkway✳ (see 03209)

Leschi Park (02700)

Licton Springs Park (03347)✳ ❧

Lincoln Park (02728) (Williams Point Park,
West Seattle Park)

Madrona Park (02702)✳

Magnolia Boulevard (including Dravus Street, Thorndyke Ave W, Thorndyke Park, and Ursula Judkins Viewpoint)✳

Magnolia Park (Magnolia Bluffs Park)

Marshall Park (see Admiral Phelps Park (02705), which was located nearby)

McGraw Square (02727)✳ ✌

Miller Playfield (02709)✳ ✌ (Pendleton Miller Playground)

Montlake Boulevard (02722)✳ (University Extension)

Mount Baker Boulevard (03209)✳

Mount Baker Park (see 03209)

Observatory Courts

Pioneer Square (Pioneer Place)

Pritchard Island Beach (portion of Pritchard Island Park)

Puget Boulevard Commons (02723) (portion of West Seattle Parkway)

Puget Park (portion of West Seattle Parkway)

Queen Anne Boulevard (Queen Anne Hill Parkway)

Rainier Beach Playfield
(see Dunlap Canyon Playfield)

Rainier Playfield (Columbia Playfield)

Ravenna Boulevard

Ravenna Park (02693)

Roanoke Park

Rogers Playfield (Denny Fuhrman Playground)

Salmon Bay Park (existing at time of 1908 plan and included in system)

Schmitz Boulevard (02719)✳ ✌ (partially vacated)

Schmitz Preserve Park (02719)✳ ✌ (Schmitz Dell Park)

17th Avenue NE (University Boulevard)

Seward Park (02724)✳ ✌

Sierra Place (see 03209)

South Park Playground (sited 7 blocks to the north by Olmsted)

Southwest Queen Anne Greenbelt (portion of Queen Anne Hill Parkway)

Sturgus Park (Beacon Park, existing parkland that was incorporated into the system)

Sunset Hill Park (Ballard Bluff Park)

Union Station Square✌ (King Street Station Park)

University of Washington campus (00346 and 02739)✳ ✌ (Alaska-Yukon-Pacific Exposition)

Van Asselt Playfield (Beacon Hill Playfield) (Located by Olmsted adjacent to Van Asselt Elementary)

Viretta Park (existing park located adjacent to boulevard)

Volunteer Park (02695)✳ ✌

Washington Park Arboretum (02699)✳ ❧

West Montlake Park

Woodland Park (02694)✳ ❧

Parks developed after 1940, but that realize the Olmsted Brothers' plans:

Bar-S Playground (Alki Point Park)

Duwamish Head Greenbelt (portion of Duwamish Head Parkway and Park)

Fairview Park

Franklin High School Playfield (Mount Baker Playfield)

Gas Works Park

Genesee Park and Stan Sayres Memorial Park (Headland Park)

Greg Davis Park (Longfellow Park)

Howell Park

Lake Union Park

Leschi-Lake Dell Natural Area

Longfellow Creek Natural Area

Magnolia Greenbelt (portion of Magnolia Boulevard)✳

Me-Kwa-Mooks Park (portion of Sound Bluffs Parkway)

Myrtle Edwards Park (includes Elliott Bay Park site)

Northeast Queen Anne Greenbelt (portion of Queen Anne Hill Parkway)

Northwest 60 Viewpoint

Rainier Urban Farms and Wetland (portion of Pritchard Island Park)

Terry Pettus Park

Victor Steinbrueck Park (Tunnel Park)

West Duwamish Greenbelt (Pigeon Point Park and Puget Park)

York Playground

No longer extant:

Collins Playfield (02710)✳ ❧ (also known as Rainier Avenue Playground and Hill Tract, replaced in function by Judkins Playfield, part of the original park exists as the privately maintained Wisteria Park)

Mercer Playfield (Mercer Park 02698) (removed for development of Seattle Center)

Southwest Playfield (site in South Seattle, north of Georgetown, removed for urban renewal project and replaced in function by Maple Wood Playfield)

ACKNOWLEDGMENTS

This book would not have been possible were it not for a happy confluence of events and decades of work by a number of people who have dedicated their time and energy to restoring, protecting, and promoting awareness of Seattle's Olmsted legacy. My involvement began with the efforts by Anne Knight and Jerry Arbes to make sure those of us working on a history of the Alaska-Yukon-Pacific Exposition knew about the significance of Olmsted's design for the 1909 world's fair grounds. I was the lucky writer assigned to cover that aspect of the exposition. I soon learned of the wealth of information about Seattle's Olmsted parks and boulevards Jerry and Anne have gathered and appreciate their generosity in sharing their knowledge and resources.

They introduced me to the Friends of Seattle's Olmsted Parks. While serving on that board, I was able to benefit from the decades of FSOP's efforts to identify and document Olmsted Brothers-designed and -influenced landscapes, and to help further document those stories. I have also benefited tremendously from conversations with current and former Seattle Department of Parks and Recreation staff, including Deputy Superintendent Christopher Williams, Michael Shiosaki, Donald Harris, Kathleen Conner, Karimeh Edwards, and Rae Tufts.

Facing the daunting task of pulling together a story extending over more than a century, I was lucky to have the help of a committee of knowledgeable advisors—Anne Knight, Sherrey Luetjen, Andy Mitton, and Jenifer Rees—to help me map out the narrative and to provide feedback on multiple drafts. Their insights helped make this a better book and the process much more enjoyable. My thanks, too, to David Williams, whose talent for clearing away the chaff brought the story into focus. I thoroughly enjoyed and appreciated talking through the finer points of Olmsted's work with him.

Without HistoryLink, and Marie McCaffrey in particular, I would not have had the resources or opportunity to work on a book like this. I am so glad to be part of an organization that supports the research and writing of important local stories and helps us have a deeper understanding of the story of our place.

My thanks, also, to the committee who came together to raise funds for this book: Chris and Dave Towne, Ken Bounds, Donald Harris, Doug and Sherrey Luetjen, Andy Mitton, Dewey Potter, Jenifer Rees, Beth Weir, and Jeannette Williams. Many of the committee members have played key roles in making Seattle's park system what it is today and have generously donated their time to bringing this project to fruition. Many thanks to the donors who responded with an outpouring of generosity.

Jeannette Williams went the extra mile—and then some—tracking down photographs, maps, and ephemera to illustrate the book. It was great to share the thrill of discovery with someone who enjoys it as much as I do.

The breadth and depth and geographic distribution of information available about Seattle's Olmsted park system is such that it would have been unmanageable without the dedicated efforts of members of Friends of Seattle's Olmsted Parks and the archivists and librarians who have tended to the voluminous documents produced by the Olmsted Brothers, Olmsted family members, the Board of Park Commissioners, Department of Parks and Recreation staff, and others.

The staff at the Seattle Municipal Archives, the University of Washington's Special Collections, and the Seattle Public Library's Seattle Room have collected and organized letters, plans, photographs, newspaper articles, and ephemera, and made them readily available to researchers like me. Time and again I have thanked my lucky stars for such extensive collections and the amazing archivists and librarians who tend to them.

On the East Coast, the National Park Service's Frederick Law Olmsted National Historic Site staff have scanned and made available online thousands of plans from the Olmsted Brothers' files. They have also worked with FSOP and the National Association for Olmsted Parks to make the plans related to Washington state available on OlmstedOnline.org.

Also, the Library of Congress provided microfilms of Olmsted Brothers correspondence files related to Washington state projects for the digitizing and indexing project funded by the Washington State Department of Transportation. With the help of Mary Hammer, Patrick Williams, and June Timmons from the Washington State Archives, those documents are now available online at the Washington State Digital Archives. Such remarkably easy access to those documents made this project possible.

It was a pleasure, as always, to work with Petyr Beck from Documentary Media. His enthusiasm for telling stories and experience in making beautiful books are a gift to a writer. Judy Gouldthorpe's expertise and eagle eye are always appreciated, as is Jon Cannell's uncanny ability to perfectly complement the story with his design.

And last, but certainly not least, thank you to my family—Brad, Henry, and Elliot—for all the time you've held the photo books on walking tours of Olmsted parks, volunteered at park events, and encouraged me when my confidence flagged. You are my favorite people to walk with along an Olmsted park path.

SPONSORS

Jerry Arbes and Anne Knight

Arboretum Foundation

Geraldine Armbruster

Thatcher Bailey

Robert Baines

Robert Barlett

Christopher Bayley

Douglas Bayley

Berger Partnership

Mark Blitzer

Kenneth Bounds and Linda Gorton

Paula Becker and Barry Brown
  in memory of Hunter Brown

Kathleen Conner and Steve Butler

Wu Wen Chu

Bessie Clark

David and Jane Cottrell

Andrew Goulding and Barbara Culp

Jared Smith and Karen Daubert

Eliza Davidson

Tanya DeMarsh-Dodson

Paul Dunn

Patrick and Susan Dunn

Hugh and Jane Ferguson Foundation

Fred and Kimberly Fishback

Joanne Foster

Barbara Freeman

Friends of Cheasty

Friends of Seattle's Olmsted Parks

James Gale

Donald and Gayle Harris

C. David Hughbanks

Timothy Jackins

Douglas Jackson

Fred Jarrett

Maryanne Tagney and David Terry Jones

Daniel Kerlee

Frank Klaus

Anita Bryant and Thomas Krese

Penny and John Kriese

Douglas and Sherrey Luetjen

Andy Mitton and Jesse Johnson

Kathleen Colombo and Patrick Morton

Sue Nicol

Jenifer Rees

Mark and Christine Reis

Mike Repass

Jeannette Reynolds

Michael and Edith Ruby

Seattle Garden Club

Megan Smith

Seattle Parks Foundation

Seattle Parks and Recreation

Stephanie Pulakis Stafford and William Stafford

Chris and David Towne

Volunteer Park Trust

Jennifer Wah

John Wott

Scott and Jennifer Wyatt

Green Lake Park pedestrian and bicycle path, 2015.

SOURCES

ARTICLES

Burgess, Patricia. "The Expert's Vision: The Role of Design in the Historical Development of City Planning," *Journal of Architectural and Planning Research,* Summer 1991, pp. 91-106.

Crawford, Andrew Wright. "The Development of Park Systems in American Cities," *The Annals of the American Academy of Political and Social Science,* March 1905, pp. 16-32.

Hundley, Walter R. "Parks for Seattle's Future," *Puget Soundings,* October 1979, pp. 32-34.

Mische, E.T. "In Memoriam," *Park and Recreation,* April 1920, pp. 52-54.

"Observations on the Progress of Improvements in Street Plans, with Special Reference to the Parkway Proposed to Be Laid out in Brooklyn," in *Annual Reports of the Park Commissioners, 1861-1873.* Brooklyn: Board of Park Commissioners, 1873. pp. 7-21.

Peterson, Sarah Jo. "Voting for Play: The Democratic Potential of Progressive Era Playgrounds." *The Journal of the Gilded Age and Progressive Era,* vol. 3, no. 2, 2004, pp. 145–175.

"Report of the Landscape Architects and Superintendents," in *Annual Reports of the Park Commissioners, 1861-1873.* Brooklyn: Board of Park Commissioners, 1873. pp. 173-202.

Scheper, George L. "The Reformist Vision of Frederick Law Olmsted and the Poetics of Park Design," *The New England Quarterly,* September 1989, pp. 369-402.

Streatfield, David C. "Parks from Seattle's Past," *Puget Soundings,* October 1979, pp. 26-31.

BOOKS

Beveridge, Charles E., ed. *Frederick Law Olmsted: Writings on Landscape, Culture, and Society.* New York: Library of America, 2015.

Blackford, Mansel G. *The Lost Dream: Businessmen and City Planning on the Pacific Coast, 1890-1920.* Columbus: Ohio State University Press, 1993.

Brown, Frederick L. *The City Is More than Human: An Animal History of Seattle.* Seattle: University of Washington Press, 2016.

Chudacoff, Howard B., Judith E. Smith, and Peter C. Baldwin. *The Evolution of American Urban Society.* New York: Routledge, 2016.

Cranz, Galen. *The Politics of Park Design: A History of Urban Parks in America.* Cambridge, MA: The MIT Press, 1982.

Hockaday, Joan. *Greenscapes: Olmsted's Pacific Northwest.* Pullman: Washington State University Press, 2009.

Plan of Seattle: Report of the Municipal Plans Commission Submitting the Report of Virgil G. Bogue, Engineer. Seattle: Lowman & Hanford Co., 1911.

Rauch, John H. *Public Parks: Their Effects on the Moral, Physical and Sanitary Condition of the Inhabitants of Large Cities.* Chicago: S. C. Griggs & Company, 1869.

Reps, John W. *Cities of the American West: A History of Frontier Urban Planning.* Princeton: Princeton University Press, 1979.

Schmitz, Henry. *The Long Road Travelled: An Account of Forestry of the University of Washington.* Seattle: Arboretum Foundation, 1973.

Schuyler, David. *The New Urban Landscape: The Redefinition of City Form in Nineteenth-Century America.* Baltimore: The Johns Hopkins University Press, 1986.

Schuyler, David, Gregor Kaliss, eds. *The Last Great Projects, 1890-1895,* Volume IX of *The Papers of Frederick Law Olmsted.* Baltimore: Johns Hopkins University Press, 2015.

Wilson, William H. *The City Beautiful Movement.* Baltimore: The Johns Hopkins University Press, 1989.

Wilson, William H. *Shaper of Seattle: Reginald Heber Thomson's Pacific Northwest.* Pullman: Washington State University Press, 2009.

LEGISLATION

"Charter of the City of Seattle," adopted October 1, 1890.

"Charter of the City of Seattle," adopted March 3, 1896.

City of Seattle Ordinance No. 36, "An Ordinance concerning Seattle cemetery and City sexton," signed by mayor January 3, 1873.

City of Seattle Ordinance No. 571, "An Ordinance for the purpose of converting Seattle Cemetery into a public park," passed July 9, 1884.

City of Seattle Ordinance No. 642, "An Ordinance creating Washelli cemetery and setting apart and dedicating the grounds for the same," passed February 6, 1885.

City of Seattle Ordinance No. 877, "An Ordinance converting Washelli cemetery in the City of Seattle into a public park, and providing for the removal of the bodies of persons burned therein and for the purchase by the city of the burial lots therein owned by private persons," passed October 4, 1887.

City of Seattle Ordinance No. 5740, "An Ordinance appropriating money to pay certain audited claims and ordering the payment thereof," December 18, 1899.

City of Seattle Ordinance No. 6907, "An Ordinance naming the public park now known as City Park, 'Volunteer Park'," passed May 20, 1901.

City of Seattle Ordinance No. 20841, "An Ordinance providing for the setting aside and designating as a boulevard and parkway University Boulevard, from East Forty-fifth Street to Ravenna Boulevard, and Ravenna Boulevard, from University Boulevard to Fifteenth Avenue Northeast, all in the City of Seattle," passed April 26, 1909.

City of Seattle Ordinance No. 27883, "An Ordinance accepting a deed from J. W. Clise, Anna H. Clise, his wife; William Nottingham and Eloise H. Nottingham, his wife; Flora B. Smith, widow of Lyman C. Smith, deceased; Burns Lyman Smith, son of Lyman C. Smith, deceased, and Virginia H. Smith, his wife, and Flora Bernice Smith, a minor daughter of Lyman C. Smith, deceased, to lands situate in the S 1/2 of the SE 1/4 of Section 22, Township 25 North, Range 3 East, W. M.," passed August 28, 1911.

City of Seattle Ordinance No. 65130, "An Ordinance relating to and authorizing the Board of Park Commissioners to enter into an agreement with the Board of Regents of the University of Washington for the establishment and maintenance of an arboretum and botanical garden in Washington Park," passed December 24, 1934.

Seattle City Council Resolution No. 33, "A Resolution declaring that it is the intention of the City Council to authorize the construction by The Queen City Cycle Club of a cycle path," adopted August 3, 1896.

Seattle City Council Resolution No. 868, "A Resolution declaring that it is the intention of the City Council to adopt the plan of parks, parkways and playgrounds, as outlined in the report and map prepared by Olmsted Brothers of Boston and known as their primary plan for the beautification of the City of Seattle, be and the same is hereby in the main adopted by the City of Seattle as a guide in the acquirement of land for parks, parkways and play grounds," adopted November 16, 1903.

Laws of Washington Territory 1869, Local and Private Laws, "An Act to Incorporate the City of Seattle," approved December 2, 1869.

Laws of Washington Territory 1875, Local and Private Laws, "An Act to Amend an Act to Incorporate the City of Seattle," approved December 2, 1869.

Laws of Washington 1907, Chapter 3, "Providing for the Sale of Certain Shore Lands and Creating Alaska-Yukon-Pacific Exposition Fund," passed February 1, 1907.

Archival Collections

Board of Park Commissioners to George Cotterill, September 5, 1902, Box 7, Folder 18, George Cotterill Papers, Access. No. 0038-0001, University of Washington Special Collections.

Board of Park Commissioners Minutes, Volumes 1-7, Record Series 5800-01, Seattle Municipal Archives.

City of Seattle Comptroller File No. 36099, "Request of Board of Park Commissioners for setting aside of Lakeside Avenue for park and parkway purposes," filed January 9, 1909, Seattle Municipal Archives.

Incoming Letters, Olmsted Brothers, 1903-1910, Box 4, Folder 25, University of Washington Board of Regents Records 1862-1965, Access. No. 78-103, University of Washington Special Collections.

"Long Range Guidelines and Design Improvement Program for the Restoration of the Lake Washington Boulevard: Working Papers Prepared by EDAW, Inc. and Walmsley & Co., Inc., May 1986 for City of Seattle Department of Parks & Recreation," unpublished report, Seattle Department of Parks & Recreation Files.

[McGilvra, John J.] to Editor, February 25, 1901, Box 2, Folder 12, John J. McGilvra Papers, Access. No. 4806-001, University of Washington Special Collections.

Olmsted Brothers Papers, Access. No. 0170-001, Special Collections, University of Washington Libraries. Available online via the Washington State Digital Archives, http://digitalarchives.wa.gov.

Olmsted John C. to Sophie Olmsted, letters dated 1903-1910, John C. Olmsted Papers, Frances Loeb Library, Harvard Design School, Harvard University, Cambridge, Massachusetts.

Parks History Files, 1892-1985, Boxes 19-52, Don Sherwood Parks History Collection, 1876-1979, Record Series 5801-01, Seattle Municipal Archives.

Seattle Job Files, Olmsted Associates Records, 1863-1971, MSS52571, Library of Congress. Available online via the Washington State Digital Archives, http://digitalarchives.wa.gov.

A Seattle Legacy: The Olmsted Parks conference materials, 1981, Seattle Room, Seattle Public Library.

Taylor, James. "Report to the Board of Park Commissioners," General File 992366, Box 18, Folder 3, General Files, Record Series 1802-04, Seattle Municipal Archives.

"Too Little! And Too Late?: Public Beaches, Parks & Parkways," 1951?, Box 1, Folder 3, Planning Commission, Series 432, King County Archives.

Wright, Edgar J. "Tooling for a Comprehensive Plan: Chairman's Report, 1950-1951," Box 1, Folder 6, Planning Commission, Series 432, King County Archives.

Newspapers

The Seattle Times and *Seattle Post-Intelligencer* (both searchable online) provided extensive reporting about development of the Seattle park system. Other local newspapers referenced included *The Seattle Republican* and *The Seattle Star*.

Online Resources

"Annexed Cities," Seattle Municipal Archives website, accessed June 1, 2019: http://www.seattle.gov/cityarchives/seattle-facts/quick-city-info#annexedcities.

"The Design Principles of Frederick Law Olmsted," National Association for Olmsted Parks website, accessed May 20, 2018: http://www.olmsted.org/the-olmsted-legacy/olmsted-theory-and-design-principles/design-principles.

"Historic Overview," Historic Columbia Gorge Highway website, National Park Service website, accessed January 14, 2018: https://www.nps.gov/tps/how-to-preserve/currents/columbia/historic.htm.

King County Recorder, Plats and Surveys, 1870-Present, Washington State Archives, Digital Archives, accessed September 10, 2018: https://digitalarchives.wa.gov/Collections/TitleInfo/2067.

Lange, Greg. "Stock market tumble on May 5, 1893, triggers Panic of 1893, sending King County and the Puget Sound region into a four-year depression," HistoryLink.org, accessed January 20, 2019.

Olmsted Park System of Louisville National Register of Historic Places Nomination, January 1981, NPGallery Digital Asset Management System website, accessed December 1, 2018: https://npgallery.nps.gov/AssetDetail/f054b939-5487-408b-b897-a9bb62193cf4.

"Playground Association of America," Play and Playground Encyclopedia website, accessed January 30, 2018: https://www.pgpedia.com/p/playground-association-america.

United States. Congress. House. Committee on Interior and Insular Affairs. Subcommittee on Public Lands. *Olmsted Heritage Landscapes Act: Hearing Before the Subcommittee on Public Lands of the Committee on Interior and Insular Affairs, House of Representatives, Ninety-ninth Congress, First Session on H.R. 37 … Hearing Held In Washington, DC, March 26, 1985* (Washington: U.S. G.P.O., 1987), available online via the Hathi Trust Digital Library (catalog.hathitrust.org/Record/008515914).

Volunteer Park Landmark Nomination, February 2011, Friends of Seattle's Olmsted Parks website, accessed November 10, 2018: https://s3.amazonaws.com/seattleolmsted/links/8/Volunteer_Park_Landmark_Nomination.pdf?1379912612.

"Washington Park Arboretum Historic Review, September 2003," University of Washington Botanic Gardens website accessed October 3, 2012: http://depts.washington.edu/uwbg/docs/arbhistory.pdf.

REPORTS

Annual Reports, Boxes 1-3, 1802-H6, Parks Department Annual Reports, Seattle Municipal Archives.

"Comprehensive Report and Recommendation of the Board of Park Commissioners to the City Council of Seattle for Improvements for the Park System," December 19, 1923, Box 1, Folder 11, Parks Department Annual Reports, Record Series 1802-H6, Seattle Municipal Archives.

Olmsted Brothers to E. F. Blaine, July 1, 1903, Job #2690, Seattle Park System. From Library of Congress, Olmsted Associates Records, 1863-1971, MSS52571, Washington State Digital Archives, http://digitalarchives.wa.gov.

Olmsted Brothers to J. M. Frink, January 25, 1908, Job #2690, Seattle Park System. From Library of Congress, Olmsted Associates Records, 1863-1971, MSS52571, Washington State Digital Archives, http://digitalarchives.wa.gov.

[Olmsted, J. C.] to J. T. Heffernan, October 4, 1910, Job #2690, Seattle Park System. From Library of Congress, Olmsted Associates Records, 1863-1971, MSS52571, Washington State Digital Archives, http://digitalarchives.wa.gov.

Parks, Playgrounds and Boulevards of Seattle, Washington (Seattle: Board of Park Commissioners, 1909).

"Report of the Landscape Architects and Superintendents," in *Annual Reports of the Park Commissioners, 1861-1873*. Brooklyn: Board of Park Commissioners, 1873. pp. 173-202.

Report of the Park Board, Portland, Oregon, 1903, With the Report of Messrs. Olmsted Bros., Landscape Architects, Outlining a System of Parkways, Boulevards and Parks for the City of Portland (Portland: Park Board?, 1903), available online via the Hathi Trust Digital Library (https://catalog.hathitrust.org/Record/012517813).

CREDITS

Cover: Dean Forbes

Inside front cover: National Park Service, Frederick Law Olmsted National Historic Site, 02721-05

1: Seattle Municipal Archives, 29282

2: Seattle Municipal Archives, 30258

6: Seattle Municipal Archives, 29984

8: King County Archives

9a: Library of Congress, 2010645986

9b: Jennifer Johnston, Mount Auburn Cemetery

10 and 11a: National Park Service, Frederick Law Olmsted National Historic Site, 00502-5

11b: Tacoma Public Library, TPL-601

12: National Park Service, Frederick Law Olmsted National Historic Site, 00700-z13

13a: J&A Collections

13b: J&A Collections

14: University of Washington Libraries, Special Collections, UWN22

15: Seattle Public Library, spl_shp_40898

16a: Seattle Public Library, spl_shp_22853

16b: J&A Collections

17a: Seattle Municipal Archives, 28967

17b: J&A Collections

18a: National Park Service, Frederick Law Olmsted National Historic Site, 1-FLO

18b: Library of Congress, 53299

18c: Frances Loeb Library Harvard University Graduate School of Design

19: National Park Service, Frederick Law Olmsted National Historic Site, FRLA 45394

20a: Tacoma Public Library, 2905

20b: Seattle Municipal Archives, 28963

21: University of Washington Libraries, Special Collections, A. Curtis 16395

22: Seattle Public Library, spl_shp_5187

23: Seattle Municipal Archives, 30730

24: *The American Monthly Review of Reviews,* December 1897, University of Washington Libraries

25: Museum of History & Industry, SHS2962

26: Seattle Municipal Archives, Box 1, Folder 3, Record Series 1802-H6

28a: Museum of History & Industry, SHS16851

28b: National Park Service, Frederick Law Olmsted National Historic Site, 02706-01-ph74

30: University of Washington Libraries, Special Collections, UW 40246

31: J&A Collections

33: Frances Loeb Library, Harvard University Graduate School of Design

34: National Oceanic and Atmospheric Administration

35: Seattle Municipal Archives, 5801-01-53-01-004

36: Seattle Municipal Archives, 5801-01-53-01-005

37: National Park Service, Frederick Law Olmsted National Historic Site, 02690-03

38: National Park Service, Frederick Law Olmsted National Historic Site, 02931

39: J&A Collections

40a: Double half-length portrait of John Charles and Sophia White Olmsted, location unknown, undated, Historic New England

40b: J&A Collections

41: National Park Service, Frederick Law Olmsted National Historic Site, 00916-01-ph25

42: Boston Public Library, 10_07_000292a

43a: J&A Collections

43b: J&A Collections

44a: Seattle Municipal Archives, 29547

44b: J&A Collections

45a: National Park Service, Frederick Law Olmsted National Historic Site, 2690-01-ph29

45b: National Park Service, Frederick Law Olmsted National Historic Site, 2690-01-ph33

46: Library of Congress, 93506477

47: Library of Congress, 2010587004

48: National Park Service, Frederick Law Olmsted National Historic Site, 2690-06

49: Seattle Municipal Archives, 31004

50a: National Park Service, Frederick Law Olmsted National Historic Site, 02696-01-ph20

50b: National Park Service, Frederick Law Olmsted National Historic Site, 02706-01-ph75

51a: University of Washington Libraries, Special Collections, UW 5490

51b: Museum of History and Industry, 1987.69.2

53: National Park Service, Frederick Law Olmsted National Historic Site, 02706-01-ph58

54a: J&A Collections

54b: J&A Collections

55: National Park Service, Frederick Law Olmsted National Historic Site, 00346-09

56: University of Washington Libraries, Special Collections, UW 40248

57: Library of Congress, Olmsted Associates Records, 1863-1971, MSS52571, Job #2690, Microfilm Roll 95

58: Seattle Municipal Archives, 29823

59: University of Washington Libraries, Special Collections, UW 4291

60: National Park Service, Frederick Law Olmsted National Historic Site, 02697-01-ph15

61: National Park Service, Frederick Law Olmsted National Historic Site, 02696-01-ph12

62: Seattle Municipal Archives, 178056

63: (Base map) National Park Service, Frederick Law Olmsted National Historic Site, 02690-10

64: J&A Collections

65: (Base map) National Park Service, Frederick Law Olmsted National Historic Site, 02690-10

67: Museum of History and Industry, SHS753

69: University of Washington Special Collections, UW 8571

70: Seattle Municipal Archives, 2328

71: University of Washington Libraries, UW 40251

73: J&A Collections

74: Seattle Public Library, spl_maps_34119113

75: Seattle Public Library

76a: Seattle Municipal Archives, 29445

76b: Seattle Public Library, spl_shp_40512

77a: National Park Service, Frederick Law Olmsted National Historic Site, 02691-05

77b: National Park Service, Frederick Law Olmsted National Historic Site, 02691-12

78: Seattle Municipal Archives, 30543

80: National Park Service, Frederick Law Olmsted National Historic Site, 02919

81a: Seattle Public Schools District Archives, 265-44

81b: Seattle Municipal Archives, 29378

82a: National Park Service, Frederick Law Olmsted National Historic Site, 02695-06

82b: National Park Service, Frederick Law Olmsted National Historic Site, 02695-35

83: National Park Service, Frederick Law Olmsted National Historic Site, 02695-01-ph22

84: Seattle Room, Seattle Public Library

85: Seattle Municipal Archives, 30148

87: Paul Dorpat

88: King County Archives, 219-3-21

89: National Park Service, Frederick Law Olmsted National Historic Site, 03209-01-pt1

90: Seattle Municipal Archives, 2325

91: J&A Collections

92: National Park Service, Frederick Law Olmsted National Historic Site, 02709-05

94: Seattle Municipal Archives, 6128

95a: National Park Service, Frederick Law Olmsted National Historic Site, 02708-11

95b: J&A Collections

96: Seattle Municipal Archives, 30179

97a: National Park Service, Frederick Law Olmsted National Historic Site, 02710-06

97b: Seattle Room, Seattle Public Library

98: University of Washington Special Collections, UW 40266

99: National Park Service, Frederick Law Olmsted National Historic Site, 02694-04

101: National Park Service, Frederick Law Olmsted National Historic Site, 02694-60-sh2

102: J&A Collections

103: Seattle Municipal Archives, 2613-03-001-003-001

104: Seattle Municipal Archives, 607

105: J&A Collections

107: Seattle Municipal Archives, 2390

108: (Base map) National Park Service, Frederick Law Olmsted National Historic Site, 02690-06

111a: Washington State Digital Archives

111b: Seattle Municipal Archives, 43412

112: Seattle Municipal Archives, 30188

113a: Seattle Municipal Archives, 2328

113b: Seattle Municipal Archives, 29278

115: Seattle Municipal Archives, 5801-01-30-19

116: Seattle Public Library, spl_maps_2444648_3

117: Seattle Municipal Archives, 30259

118: Seattle Municipal Archives, 30391

119a: Seattle Municipal Archives, 29856

119b: Seattle Municipal Archives, 29372

120a: University of Washington Libraries, Special Collections, UW 28620z

120b: University of Washington Libraries, Special Collections, UW 40249

122a: Seattle Municipal Archives, 2326

122b: Seattle Municipal Archives, 64050

123: J&A Collections

124: Seattle Municipal Archives, 2316

125: National Park Service, Frederick Law Olmsted National Historic Site, 00346-16

127: University of Washington Libraries, Special Collections, UW 6049

128: J&A Collections

129a: Photo by Mike Siegel, E. B. Dunn Garden Estate

129b: National Park Service, Frederick Law Olmsted National Historic Site, 03276-z1

129c: National Park Service, Frederick Law Olmsted National Historic Site, 03095-17

129d: Gerald W Williams Regional Albums (P 303), Oregon State University Special Collections & Archives Research Center, Corvallis, Oregon

130: Seattle Municipal Archives, 178408

131: Seattle Municipal Archives, 178472

132: Seattle Municipal Archives, 29712

133: Seattle Municipal Archives, 2332 and 2333

134a: PEMCO Webster & Stevens Collection, Museum of History & Industry, 1983.10.8978

134b: Seattle Municipal Archives, 30852

135: J&A Collections

137: Seattle Municipal Archives, 178735

138: Seattle Garden Club

139a: Catherine Joy Johnson

139b: J&A Collections

140: University of Washington Libraries, Special Collections, UW 40250

141a: Seattle Municipal Archives, Record Series 2615-02

141b: Seattle Municipal Archives, 30749

142: Seattle Municipal Archives, 63320

143: Seattle Municipal Archives, 30749

144: Seattle Municipal Archives, 63183

145: National Park Service, Frederick Law Olmsted National Historic Site, 00706-z10

146: Seattle Room, Seattle Public Library

147: Friends of Seattle's Olmsted Parks

148: Seattle Public Utilities and Hoffman Construction

149: Friends of Seattle's Olmsted Parks

150: Bob Baines

151a: Seattle Municipal Archives, 178729

151b: Seattle Municipal Archives, 177921

153a: Seattle Municipal Archives, 178055

153b: Seattle Municipal Archives, 108472

154: Seattle Municipal Archives, 170833

155a: Seattle Municipal Archives, 178357

155b: Bob Baines

163: Photo by TIA International Photography. Seattle Municipal Archives, 178475

176: Photo by Mike Siegel. E. B. Dunn Garden Estate

Inside back cover: Seattle Municipal Archives, 2320

INDEX

Note: Page numbers in *italics* indicate images.